MW00575673

ZX SPECTRUM GAMES CODE CLUB

Twenty fun games to type in, learn from and extend

Gary Plowman

ZX SPECTRUM GAMES CODE CLUB

First published in 2015 by Gazzapper Press

http://www.gazzapper.com

Cover design by Gary Plowman

Published By Gazzapper Press

Copyright © 2015 Gary Plowman

All rights reserved.

ISBN-10: 0993474454
ISBN-13: 978-0-993474453 (Gazzapper Press)

SPECIAL THANKS

To Gabby and Pippin for putting up with the late nights

ACKNOWLEDGEMENTS

I would like to express my gratitude to all the supporters of this book and those ZX Spectrum & BASIC coding fans that supported the idea in its early stages.

I would like to thank my partner Gabrielle for her help in testing some of the code within this book.

Thanks to my parents for buying me the ZX Spectrum for Christmas back in 80s.

Thanks to Richard Langford for the use of his 48k Spectrum graphic image.

Thanks to the larger Retro community in general who help spread the word.

Thanks to Sir Clive Sinclair for making the Sinclair ZX Spectrums.

Contents

INTRODUCTION

Before we start, let's just clarify the purpose of this book. This is not intended as an all-knowing reference book on the ins and outs of the Sinclair BASIC language. This is a book to facilitate the learning of Sinclair BASIC by typing in the code listings for various games, the added benefit of which is that you get to enjoy your efforts in the form of some 'old school' gaming. As you progress through the book, we do less explaining so as not to bore you. There are many different types of games in this book, so I hope there is something of interest for everyone.

Perhaps some of you want to introduce a younger generation to the glory days of early micro computing with a machine that you grew up with. Or you may wish to provide a local **Code Club** with easy to learn activities for building fun games, without the need to be a skilled artist, boffin or whiz kid. Or perhaps you are a ZX fan and have gotten yourself one of those new Bluetooth ZX Spectrums, either way we hope you have fun using this book.

As a teenager I benefitted from learning BASIC programming and the experience opened doors to many possibilities, it gave me a passion for computing and coding in general. Today, I am involved in desktop, web and mobile coding for both game development, business applications and Internet startups. Everyone has to start somewhere and it's never too late or too early to learn to code.

So why Sinclair BASIC?

The Sinclair BASIC language is one of the gateways to professional coding that many successful British and European programmers started with before going on to program amazing games and utilities, during the 1980s. All this was done in less than 48k of RAM. Some examples of the these are *RARE* (aka Ultimate Play the Game, aka ACG), *The Oliver Twins* (Dizzy series), *Codemasters*, and many more.

BASIC stands for **B**eginners **A**ll **P**urpose **S**ymbolic **I**nstruction **C**ode, so it's perfect for beginners learning to code. It is friendly and fun to learn and the commands are logical and clearly named after the function they perform.

Sinclair BASIC teaches logic, how to perform decisions and structure your code but only for simple concepts. It helps with basic math skills – and you do not need be a math Guru to learn it.

The BASIC ROM (Read Only Memory) is the operating system of the Sinclair machine and is setup in such a way so it will not allow illegal code to be entered. Each line is validated by the ROM, so after entering a line you will hear an acceptance beep sound for a line entered correctly. If the line is incorrect, then a lower tone sound is used and the system prompts you to fix any incorrect code.

A note of thanks must go to the Sinclair guys and especially Steve Vickers and the rest of the guys at Nine Tiles Ltd for creating Sinclair BASIC.

What do you need before we start?

Any of the following configurations is fine for starting quickly:

a) A Real ZX Spectrum: e.g. ZX Spectrum 16k, 48k, 48K+, 128K or any further model.

b) A computer that can run an emulator: Example of some emulators for various platforms...

Windows:	ZX Spin, Spectaculator, Speccy plus many more.
Mac OS:	Fuse
Linux/Unix:	Fuse
iOS/Android:	Spectaculator, Fuse, Speccy, Marvin
Chrome/FF:	There are a couple of online emulators that will work from a browser. Using Google will lead you to these, but here are two examples I know of that will work in your browser.

http://jsspeccy.zxdemo.org

http://torinak.com/qaop

c) Another good option is the new Recreated ZX Spectrum (Bluetooth) which works with Android and iOS.

For beginners to the ZX Spectrum I would suggesting coding in **128k mode** as this allows for typed commands and does not require combination key-presses required by 48k mode. But if you are up to the challenge or you want a nostalgia hit then by all means go for 48k or 16k mode.

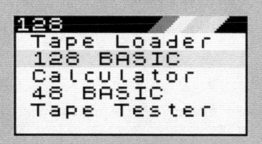

Quick Start

If you want to dive into writing your code now, and you have one of the options above ready-to-go, then by all means you can skip this next section and begin coding one of the games right now.

Basic Commands

Some of the most common commands that we will be using are PRINT, IF , GOTO, GO SUB, DIM and LET. I will only give you an overview of each of these as this is a book for learning-by-doing and not meant to be used like a manual. Having too much technical jargon to read gets boring after a while. We need to be hitting the fleshy keys of the Spectrum 48k or the plastic clicky tones of the Spectrum 128k models or the your preferred emulator.

Here is the obligatory "hello world" example that is present in nearly all coding books.

```
10 PRINT AT 10,5; "Hello World"
```

Hit Enter at the end of the line to save it in memory, then type RUN and hit enter again to see it working.

The breakdown of the above example code is...

10	=	Line numbering (sequence order of the program)
PRINT	=	PRINTing on the screen (easy!)
AT y,x	=	Telling the program the coordinates to PRINT at where y is vertical axis and x is horizontal
;	=	Allows for a new sub function or for the text to print
"Hello World"	=	Your text contents

PRINT will populate text or special graphics characters (i.e. UDGs) on the screen at the position you specify. The ZX Spectrum workable screen is 32 character columns (0 to 31) wide and 22 lines long (0 to 21). The AT (operand) part of the command is telling the command to place items at Y (line) , X (Column). There are 2 additional lines but these are not used with the standard PRINT command.

The following sub functions will work inline with the PRINT command:

INK <0-7>	Sets the foreground colour for the pen which prints all text and graphics
PAPER <0-7>	Sets the colour for the paper background of the main screen
INVERSE <1 or 0>	Prints and Inverse of the current INK and PAPER setup
OVER <1 or 0>	Turns on / off Overprinting on the screen
FLASH <1 or 0>	Flash with repeatedly alternate between the current and inverse colours
BRIGHT <1 or 0 or 8>	Brighter versions of the colors 1 – 6 (for INK and PAPER) 8 is transparent
TAB #	Moves across horizontally from left to right # spaces

E.g. PRINT INK 2; AT 10,10;"Test"; TAB 16;PAPER 1;INK 7;FLASH 1;"Print"

As you can see you can have almost any combination of those commands on a PRINT statement.

Line Numbering

It is good practice to leave adequate gaps in numbering your code lines so you can enter additional commands at a later stage. I would suggest for your own programs to step in increments of 10 at least. So line 10, then line 20 and so on. Sinclair BASIC can have a maximum of 9999 lines but lines can contain multiple statements when separated by a colon ":", so commands can run into tens of thousands.

128k Mode and Line Numbers

The 128k spectrum mode has another feature that is handy for new coders. If your program is missing a section and you did not make enough space for the commands, you can run RENUMBER and it will re-organise the program line numbers. There are limitations to this but we need not be concerned about those at this early stage.

UDGs (User Definable Graphics)

You will learn how to make your own graphics with ease! So you can return to some of the programs in this book and add your own graphics to enhance and extend them.

Machine Code

For the purposes of this book, machine code would be a little difficult to grasp. So we will not be covering it here. However, signup for our alerts at Gazzapper.com as we may release updated versions of some of the games with small routines of machine code included.

So what is a 'Type-in Listing'?

In the earlier days of micro computing, magazines would publish 'listings' or 'type-in listings' for young enthusiasts (aka coders / programmers) to sit down and type in at their keyboards from the comfort of their bedrooms. Some listings would be misprinted or would contain bugs causing the user to be frustrated and furious with the author. If you couldn't fix the bugs, you were stuck with code that didn't run having spent hours typing them.

Well I am happy to say I have written and tested all the listings so that they do work and any issues can worked through via the new Facebook group I have setup called **ZX Spectrum Code Club**. Or if you are already a member of a ZX Spectrum group simply post your questions there (if the rules allow).

The listings were coded in a way to make the most of the speed limitations of Sinclair BASIC (within reason) so that the games are playable and hopefully fun too. The structure is made to be easy to follow and although not perfect, it will allow the user to follow what is going on inside each game. The structure of the games are kept similar so that you become familiar with them and also provides a simple template to use for your own creations.

A great feature of Sinclair BASIC is that the ROM validates the majority of the code before accepting the statements. In case you missed it earlier, ROM stands for Read Only Memory and it contains the operating system and various routines required by BASIC.

Although REM statements are not required for the running of the programs it is good practice to provide these, as the more code you add into a program the more comments are needed. Especially for the user to refer to whenever editing or extending the code at a future date. They can also be useful as visual dividers between sections of your program, making it easier to read.

Sinclair BASIC is not the fastest of programming languages but it is one of the easiest to learn and it's great fun. Without going into too much technical details a user can speed up any of the Spectrum emulators by increasing the emulator running speed from the standard 3.54MHz to x2 speed or higher in the options.

Emulator keyboard mapping

When using an emulator over a real Spectrum machine there are a few intricacies that should be pointed out in relation to keyboard mappings. Below is a real 48k Spectrum keyboard layout.

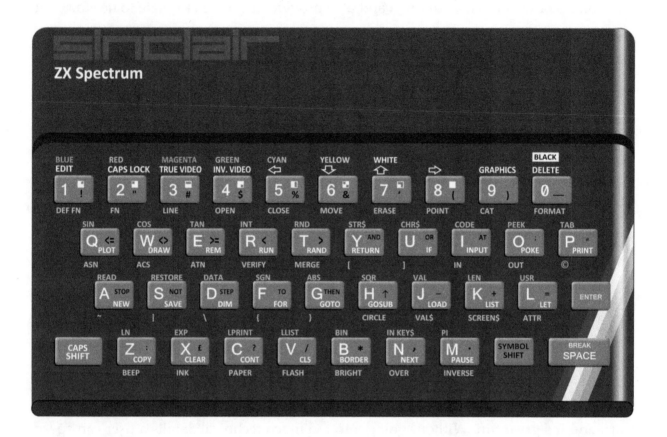

Selecting symbols such as quotes and * etc might be different on your PC / MAC keyboard than that of the emulator. This may be the case for some keyboards and emulators. You can see above that certain symbols will be different on your keyboard.

Standard Keyboard Equivalents for Sinclair Emulators

Below is a list of how some of the mappings might differ. Keep in mind that some emulators might use Alt instead of Ctrl for some of these mappings.

* (asterisk)	=	Ctrl and B	; (semi colon)	=	Alt Gr and O
(	=	Ctrl and 8	: (colon)	=	Alt Gr and Z
)	=	Ctrl and 9	Delete	=	Shift and 0 (zero)
" (quotes)	=	Ctrl and P	Graphic Mode	=	Shift and 9
. (full stop)	=	Alt Gr and M	Break / Quit	=	Shift and Space
, (comma)	=	Alt Gr and n	Extended Mode	=	Shift and Ctrl

Note: Alt Gr is the right Alt key

If you get stuck of run into any issues then submit your query to one of the many ZX Spectrum Facebook groups.

Saving your Type-Ins

This is relatively straightforward for emulator users – Just save a **snapshot** (.sna) file, but for the 'real' machine users you need an old school tape recorder and a blank C15, C30, C60 or C90 cassette. To save your Type-in Press 'Play & Record' on your tape deck (with ear and mic connected) and use SAVE "<Typein Name>" LINE 10.

ZX SPECTRUM GAMES CODE CLUB

Using a MicroDrive

Saving to a MicroDrive or emulated MicroDrive can be done like so:

SAVE *"m";1;"My Program"

You can then verify the save using:

VERIFY *"m";1;"My Program"

To remove a program just use:

ERASE "m";1;"My Program"

To Load a program:

LOAD *"m";1;"My Program"

To view contents (catalogue) of a MicroDrive disk:

CAT 1 or CAT

(Note: CAT is also used with the 128k+3 model)

MicroDrive LOAD * and SAVE * can be appended with the suffix CODE, SCREEN$ and LINE #, similar to the standard LOAD and SAVE commands.

Game Loop Basics

The Game Loop is the part of your game where all the action happens and runs repeatedly until the game is over. It follows a certain structure or sequence of events. This structure is not set in stone, but a simple example is shown below of how a Game Loop fits into your code.

---- Setup : Graphic UDGs (a.k.a Sprites) or loading data

---- Initialise: Key variables, strings and arrays

---- Menu / Start Screen for Game

---- **Game Loop:**

    ---- **Process Input / Keypresses**

    ---- **Updating positions / AI updates etc**

    ---- **Draw / Print Screen items**

    ---- **Repeat Loop**

---- End / Quit Game

I have used this type structure for most of the games in this book. I hope you find that the format helps you get your head around what a Game Loop does and how it should be used.

Tip: Pressing 'Shift and Space' will BREAK / QUIT a running program.

How to use this Book

You can code or type in these listings in any order you wish. Some commands or newer concepts though may not be explained as they may have been dealt with in a previous listing but that is fine. You will get there eventually. Remember this is for fun so if a certain game is not of interest to you feel free to skip it.

Also here is a very handy space character rule for the printed book, each 12 characters is appox. 3cm.

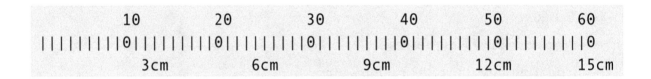

Scan / copy and print it or just refer back to if you need it for calculating spaces in the code listings. You can also make your own. The listings are mono-spaced so it should be easy to use or work out spaces.

Some Handy Tips when Typing in code...

1) *To quicken up data entry for Type-Ins you could ask a friend or a family member to read out the code listing to you line by line.*

2) *Another method is to use a ruler or another book to hide the lines you haven't yet typed in.*

3) *Always double-check the line number is correct! Lots of people make typos when typing numbers out.*

So without further delay, start typing in our games!

TIC TAC TOE
OR
NOUGHTS AND CROSSES

So let's start with a simple game. Tic Tac Toe, or Noughts and Crosses, is a simple and a fairly universal game. Most people have played this at least once before, using pencil and paper. Many school copy books were littered with these games.

Players: 2

Rules: Player 1 tries to get a row of Xs and Player 2 tries to get a row of Os.

Controls: Keys 1 to 9 will pick your square on the grid. See grid of positions below.

1   2   3

4   5   6

7   8   9

```
 10 REM **********ZX CODE CLUB***************
 15 REM * Tic-Tac-Toe or Noughts and Crosses *
 20 REM ********** Gary Plowman ************
 30 INK 7: PAPER 6: BORDER 7: CLS : LET ply=1: LET win=0: DIM
a(9,2): LET sq=0
 40 GO SUB 90
 50 GO TO 300
 60 REM *********** DRAW BOARD
 90 PRINT AT 2,10; INK 1;"Tic Tac Toe"
110 PLOT INK 5;100,40: DRAW INK 5;0,100
```

```
 120 PLOT INK 5;150,40: DRAW INK 5;0,100
 130 PLOT INK 5;65,70: DRAW INK 5;120,0
 140 PLOT INK 5;65,110: DRAW INK 5;120,0
 160 REM State 1=player 1, 2=Player 2
 175 INK 5: PLOT 50,170: DRAW -40,-40: PLOT 10,170: DRAW 40,-
40
 180 CIRCLE INK 4;220,150,20
 190 PRINT ; INK 0; PAPER 3;AT 14,0;"1 2 3";AT 15,0;"4 5 6";AT
16,0;"7 8 9"
 210 RETURN
 300 REM ******* Test Press
 310 PRINT AT 18,1; INK 7; PAPER 6-ply;"PLAYER ";ply;" Choose
Square 1 - 9"
 320 LET i$=INKEY$
 330 IF i$>="1" AND i$<="9" THEN LET square=VAL i$: GO SUB
1000
 340 IF i$="" THEN GOTO 320
 350 GO SUB 2000: REM ****** Test for Winning Conditions :)
 355 IF sq=9 THEN LET win=-1
 360 IF win>0 THEN PRINT AT 18,1;"PLAYER ";win;" has WON!":
BEEP .4,3: BEEP 2,10: GO TO 10
 370 IF win<0 THEN PRINT AT 18,1;"GAME DRAWN - RESTARTING":
BEEP .4,3: BEEP 2,10: GO TO 10
 400 GO TO 300
1000 REM ******* Check squares
1010 IF a(square,1)=1 OR a(square,2)=1 THEN PRINT AT 18,1; INK
3;"Square Taken Already": BEEP .3,1: GO TO 1050
1020 LET a(square,ply)=1: LET ply=ply+1: LET sq=sq+1
1025 PRINT AT 18,1; INK 4;"Good move!": BEEP .4,12
1030 IF ply=3 THEN LET ply=1
1040 GO SUB 3000: REM ******* Draw Move
1050 PRINT AT 18,1;"                       "
1090 RETURN
2000 REM ***** WINNING CONDITIONS CHECK
2010 FOR n=1 TO 2
2020 IF a(1,n)=1 AND a(2,n)=1 AND a(3,n)=1 THEN LET win=n
```

```
2030 IF a(1,n)=1 AND a(4,n)=1 AND a(7,n)=1 THEN LET win=n
2040 IF a(2,n)=1 AND a(5,n)=1 AND a(8,n)=1 THEN LET win=n
2050 IF a(3,n)=1 AND a(6,n)=1 AND a(9,n)=1 THEN LET win=n
2060 IF a(3,n)=1 AND a(5,n)=1 AND a(7,n)=1 THEN LET win=n
2070 IF a(1,n)=1 AND a(5,n)=1 AND a(9,n)=1 THEN LET win=n
2080 IF a(4,n)=1 AND a(5,n)=1 AND a(6,n)=1 THEN LET win=n
2090 IF a(7,n)=1 AND a(8,n)=1 AND a(9,n)=1 THEN LET win=n
2100 NEXT n
2110 RETURN
3000 REM ******* DRAW MOVE
3010 LET posx=80: LET posy=130: REM ***** where to draw
3020 IF square=1 THEN LET posx=80: LET posy=130
3030 IF square=2 THEN LET posx=130: LET posy=130
3040 IF square=3 THEN LET posx=180: LET posy=130
3050 IF square=4 THEN LET posx=80: LET posy=100
3060 IF square=5 THEN LET posx=130: LET posy=100
3070 IF square=6 THEN LET posx=180: LET posy=100
3080 IF square=7 THEN LET posx=80: LET posy=70
3090 IF square=8 THEN LET posx=130: LET posy=70
3100 IF square=9 THEN LET posx=180: LET posy=70
3300 IF ply=1 THEN CIRCLE INK 4;posx-10,posy-10,10
3310 IF ply=2 THEN INK 5: PLOT posx,posy: DRAW -20,-20: PLOT
posx-20,posy: DRAW 20,-20
3350 RETURN
```

Wow!
You have really
done it!

Now that you have completed your Type-In game, you can start playing it. To run a program in BASIC, type RUN at the prompt and then hit the enter key.

After you play

We will not go through every line, just the important stuff or any part I think might be harder to grasp.

So what does it all mean? Well lines 10 to 20 are just for show, the REM command is for adding any comments or remarks about the code.

```
10 REM *********************************
15 REM * Tic-Tac-Toe or Noughts and Crosses *
20 REM ********** Gary Plowman *************
```

Line 30 sets up the display of the game. INK command is the pen colour, PAPER is the main screen area and BORDER is the area outside the main screen area. The border area is rarely used and it not reached by PLOT or PRINT commands, but it can be made flash to indicate getting a hit or scoring a point.

```
30 INK 7: PAPER 6: BORDER 7: CLS : LET ply=1: LET win=0: DIM
a(9,2): LET sq=0
```

Next on that line is CLS. This means Clear the Screen and without it the PAPER command would not have made the whole of the screen area change colour. After that the LET command is used to setup variables. Variables store values to be used or changed at a later time in the code.

Arrays & Multi-dimensional Arrays

This next is part is not that difficult at all but don't worry if you don't get Arrays just yet. Arrays are tricky in the beginning, and it is best to think of them as lists of values.

Last part of line 30 is the DIM a(9,2) command (dimensional array). This is an array of variables and works like a list or spreadsheet in numerical order. But if you do not understand that maybe this will explain it better.

The first dimension can be thought of as **Column 1** which contains 9 rows of data. With the second part referring to **Column 2** with a different set of 9 rows of data.

```
DIM a(9,2) - 9 rows down with 2 columns

Column 1                Column 2
LET a(1,1)=1            LET a(1,2)=1      - Row 1
...                     ...
LET a(9,1)=9            LET a(9,2)=9      - Row 9
```

The commands above will store values in different sections of the array. An error occurs if you try to exceed the limits of the array as setup in your DIM statement. Arrays in Sinclair BASIC always start from 1 and not 0 (Zero).

GO SUB Explained

The GO SUB command means Go Subroutine. A GO SUB will allow a program to leap to the another part of the code based on the line number provided and then it can return to the previous position if a RETURN statement is encountered. This is very useful for dividing up a BASIC program into logical sections. A GO SUB is handy to keep in mind for any code extending you might want to add to any of the games. Each significant problem you run into can be separated off as GO SUB routine, which helps you keep track of your program.

Summary of the Remaining Program

Lines 90 to 210 draw the contents of the game screen.

```
90 PRINT AT 2,10; INK 1;"Tic Tac Toe"
110 PLOT INK 5;100,40: DRAW INK 5;0,100
120 PLOT INK 5;150,40: DRAW INK 5;0,100
130 PLOT INK 5;65,70: DRAW INK 5;120,0
```

```
140 PLOT INK 5;65,110: DRAW INK 5;120,0
160 REM State 1=player 1, 2=Player 2
175 INK 5: PLOT 50,170: DRAW -40,-40: PLOT 10,170: DRAW 40,-
40
180 CIRCLE INK 4;220,150,20
190 PRINT ; INK 0; PAPER 3;AT 14,0;"1 2 3";AT 15,0;"4 5 6";AT
16,0;"7 8 9"
210 RETURN
```

Lines 110 to 140 with PLOT, creating the starting points for drawing from. These lines draw the # grid for the game. PLOT command places your pen on the screen (making a dot). Then the DRAW command creates a line or arc.

Lines 175 to 190 will draw the large X and O symbols to the sides of the grid and will also print the grid for the player controls.

Lines 300 to 400 will run the main Game Loop, which is quite short for this game.

```
300 REM ******* Test Press
310 PRINT AT 18,1; INK 7; PAPER 6-ply;"PLAYER ";ply;" Choose
Square 1 - 9"
320 LET i$=INKEY$
330 IF i$>="1" AND i$<="9" THEN LET square=VAL i$: GO SUB
1000
340 IF i$="" THEN GOTO 320
350 GO SUB 2000: REM ****** Test for Winning Conditions :)
355 IF sq=0 THEN LET win=-1
360 IF win>0 THEN PRINT AT 18,1;"PLAYER ";win;" has WON!":
BEEP .4,3: BEEP 2,10: GO TO 10
370 IF win<0 THEN PRINT AT 18,1;"GAME DRAWN - RESTARTING":
BEEP .4,3: BEEP 2,10: GO TO 10
400 GO TO 300
```

Line 320 is important as it captures the keypresses of the players.

Line 330 checks to make sure the key pressed is valid (i.e. between 1 and 9)

Lines 1000 to 1090 check to ensure the chosen square within the grid is not already taken.

```
1000 REM ******* Check squares
1010 IF a(square,1)=1 OR a(square,2)=1 THEN PRINT AT 18,1; INK
3;"Square Taken Already": BEEP .3,1: GO TO 1050
1020 LET a(square,ply)=1: LET ply=ply+1 : LET sq=sq+1
1025 PRINT AT 18,1; INK 4;"Good move!": BEEP .4,12
1030 IF ply=3 THEN LET ply=1
1040 GO SUB 3000: REM ******* Draw Move
1050 PRINT AT 18,1;"                        "
1090 RETURN
```

Lines 2000 to 2110 check to see if the winning conditions were met. If a winner is found the program will announce it and the game restarts.

```
2000 REM ***** WINNING CONDITIONS CHECK
2010 FOR n=1 TO 2
2020 IF a(1,n)=1 AND a(2,n)=1 AND a(3,n)=1 THEN LET win=n
2030 IF a(1,n)=1 AND a(4,n)=1 AND a(7,n)=1 THEN LET win=n
2040 IF a(2,n)=1 AND a(5,n)=1 AND a(8,n)=1 THEN LET win=n
2050 IF a(3,n)=1 AND a(6,n)=1 AND a(9,n)=1 THEN LET win=n
2060 IF a(3,n)=1 AND a(5,n)=1 AND a(7,n)=1 THEN LET win=n
2070 IF a(1,n)=1 AND a(5,n)=1 AND a(9,n)=1 THEN LET win=n
2080 IF a(4,n)=1 AND a(5,n)=1 AND a(6,n)=1 THEN LET win=n
2090 IF a(7,n)=1 AND a(8,n)=1 AND a(9,n)=1 THEN LET win=n
2100 NEXT n
2110 RETURN
```

Lines 3000 to 3350 will draw a new mark on the board depending on who's turn it is.

```
3000 REM ******* DRAW MOVE
3010 LET posx=80: LET posy=130: REM ***** where to draw
3020 IF square=1 THEN LET posx=80: LET posy=130
3030 IF square=2 THEN LET posx=130: LET posy=130
3040 IF square=3 THEN LET posx=180: LET posy=130
```

```
3050 IF square=4 THEN LET posx=80: LET posy=100
3060 IF square=5 THEN LET posx=130: LET posy=100
3070 IF square=6 THEN LET posx=180: LET posy=100
3080 IF square=7 THEN LET posx=80: LET posy=70
3090 IF square=8 THEN LET posx=130: LET posy=70
3100 IF square=9 THEN LET posx=180: LET posy=70
3300 IF ply=1 THEN CIRCLE INK 4;posx-10,posy-10,10
3310 IF ply=2 THEN INK 5: PLOT posx,posy: DRAW -20,-20: PLOT
posx-20,posy: DRAW 20,-20
3350 RETURN
```

CONGRATS! You've reached LEVEL 1

So that wasn't too difficult to understand and providing you already have some prior
knowledge of BASIC you might want to consider the following exercises for extending
the game. If you need more time then move on and start coding your next game.

Suggestions for Extending (optional)

1] *Create a tally for Player One and Player Two with first to five as the winner.*
2] *Add a single player versus the computer with some basic AI
   (Artificial Intelligence)**
3] *Draw a line across the winning squares*

* Simple AI is not too difficult to implement.

ZX BREAKOUT

Based on the original Arcade game Breakout by Atari. My first experience of playing Breakout was in a pool hall near our house. I think it was the first arcade game I played that was in colour. Although later in life, I found I was duped! The game was really only black and white – the extra colours were achieved using an overlay of coloured transparent plastic. The effect on screen was quite similar to that of the ZX Spectrum's colour clash. Still, it worked its magic and I was hooked. By the way, did I mention that the two main founders of Apple created Breakout!

Players: 1

Rules: Launch the ball and keep it from falling past your bat. Eliminate 70 points worth of blocks to get to the next screen.

Controls: z = left, x = right, [space]=launch ball.

```
 10 REM *********ZX CODE CLUB***************
 15 REM * ZX BREAKOUT by G Plowman 2015      *
 20 REM ********************************
 25 GO SUB 7000
 30 INK 1: PAPER 7: BORDER 4: CLS
 35 LET lives=3
 45 REM ****** Initialising variables
 50 PRINT AT 2,10; INK 7; BRIGHT 1; PAPER 2;"ZX BREAKOUT";
BRIGHT 0; PAPER 7; INK 1;AT  6,0;"Taken from..";AT 8,0;"ZX
Spectrum Games Code Club Book": PAUSE 0
 100 GO SUB 300: REM initialise
 120 GO SUB 500: REM menu
 130 GO SUB 1000: REM main loop for game
 200 GO TO 30
```

```
 300 LET ply=2: LET win=0: DIM a(9,2): DIM d(30): LET lvl=1:
LET posy=30: LET x=10: LET time=0: LET score=0: LET timer=0:
LET mov=11: LET pos=11: LET vx=0: LET vy=0: LET speed=1: LET
ball=0: LET bx=0: LET by=0: LET score2=0
 310 LET b$=" "+CHR$ (147)+CHR$ (145)+" " : LET w$=CHR$
(146)+CHR$ (146)
 400 RETURN
 500 CLS
 510 LET w$=CHR$ (146)
 520 FOR n = 0 TO 31
 530 PRINT INK 2;AT 1,n;w$;AT 21,n;w$
 540 NEXT n
 545 FOR n = 0 TO 20:
 546 PRINT INK 2; AT n,0;w$;AT n,31;w$
 549 NEXT n
 550 RETURN
1000 REM Main Loop
1005 PRINT AT 20,x-2;" ";b$;" "
1010 LET i$=INKEY$: LET kemp=IN 31
1020 LET timer=timer+1:
1030 IF (i$="z" OR kemp=2) AND x>2 THEN LET x=x-1:
1040 IF (i$="x" OR kemp=1) AND x<29 THEN LET x=x+1
1045 IF i$="z" OR i$="x" OR kemp>0 THEN PRINT AT 20,x-2;"
";b$;" "
1050 IF (i$=CHR$ (32) OR kemp=16) AND ball=0 THEN LET
vx=(RND*1.5)-(RND*1.5): LET vy=-1: LET ball=1: LET bx=x: LET
by=19
1060 IF timer=5 THEN GO SUB 3000
1070 IF ball=1 THEN GO SUB 4000
1080 PRINT AT 0,2;"SCORE:";score;" (Lvl:";lvl;")
Lives:";lives:
2000 GO TO 1010
3000 REM draw blocks
3010 FOR n = 1 TO 20 STEP 2
3020 FOR p = 1 TO 10 STEP 2
3025 LET ir=RND*4+1
```

```
3030 PRINT AT p+2,n+4; INK 0; PAPER ir;"__":
3050 NEXT p
3060 NEXT n
3070 LET timer = 6
3100 RETURN
4000 REM **** BALL MOVE
4005 PRINT AT by,bx;" "
4010 LET bx=bx+vx: LET by=by+vy
4014 LET y$ =SCREEN$ (INT (by),INT (bx))
4015 IF y$="_" THEN LET score = score + 1: BEEP .008,vx+bx:
LET score2=score2+1: LET vy=-vy*speed
4016 IF by>=19 AND ABS (bx-x)<2 THEN LET vx=((RND*2)+1)-
((RND*2)+1): LET vy=-vy*speed: PRINT AT 20,x-2;" ";b$;" "
4020 PRINT AT by,bx; INK 2;CHR$ (144)
4040 IF bx>29 THEN LET vx=-(vx*speed)
4050 IF bx<2 THEN LET vx=-(vx*speed)
4060 IF by>=20 THEN LET ball=0: LET lives=lives-1: BORDER 2:
BEEP 1,0: BORDER 4
4070 IF by<3 THEN LET vy=-(vy*speed)
4080 IF lives=0 THEN GO SUB 5000:
4090 IF score2>=70 THEN GO SUB 6000: REM Next level:
4200 RETURN
5000 REM **** restart
5010 PRINT AT 10,5; FLASH 1; PAPER 6; INK 2;"G A M E    O V E
R"
5030 FOR n =1 TO 200
5050 NEXT n
5100 PRINT AT 12,5;"PRESS KEY TO RESTART"
5110 IF INKEY$="" THEN GO TO 5110
5120 GO TO 30
6000 REM **** NEXT LEVEL
6005 LET lvl=lvl+1: CLS : PRINT AT 10,10; FLASH 1; "L E V E L
";lvl
6010 BEEP 1,13
6020 LET timer=2
6050 FOR n=1 TO 100
```

```
6055 BEEP .001,n/10
6060 NEXT n
6070 LET score2=0
6080 LET ball=0
6100 GO TO 120
7000 REM **** CREATE UDG GRAPHICS!!
7010 FOR n = 0 TO 31
7020 READ graph
7030 POKE USR "a"+n,graph
7050 NEXT n
7060 RETURN
7190 REM ************BALL
7200 DATA BIN 00111100
7210 DATA BIN 01100110
7220 DATA BIN 01011110
7230 DATA BIN 01011110
7240 DATA BIN 01111110
7250 DATA BIN 00111100
7260 DATA BIN 00000000
7270 DATA BIN 00000000
7280 REM ************BAT left side- using full numbers
7300 DATA 252,42,41,2,252,248,0,224
7370 REM *************wall
7400 DATA 231,195,165,24,24,165,195,231
7470 REM *********** BAT right side
7480 DATA 63,84,148,64,63,31,0,7
```

What's New?

The RND function is used to generate a Random value between 0 and 1 which is multiplied by a value which determines the range of the values involved. E.g. INT(RND*10) will return an INTEGER value of RND*10, so a value between 0 and 9 as INT command rounds down a number to ZERO decimal places.

Other new parts in this listing are UDGs (User Definable Graphics) and some basic collision detection. So we will go over these briefly. Also new is the use of directional vector values stored in vx and vy. Which constantly increase or decrease the x and y values for ball movement by adding itself (vx or vy) to x or y in every loop.

```
4010 LET bx=bx+vx: LET by=by+vy
```

So what are UDGs?

UDGs stand for User Definable Graphics and they help add graphic sprites to a game. Lines 7010 to 7050 look for values to place into memory to create the UDGs. While Lines 7300 keep the data which make up the values to go into the UDG memory.

```
7010 FOR n = 0 TO 31
7020 READ graph
7030 POKE USR "a"+n,graph
7050 NEXT n
```

The READ command looks for DATA statements in your code. It reads each value within the DATA statements in order, if it runs out of data then an error occurs. So make you have all your data values entered. You can tell READ where to start from using RESTORE <data_line_number>. UDGs are graphics characters within the character set, by default they start out looking like the same as the letters A to Z. After some well thought out POKEs these letters can be changed to graphics. Each UDG character has 8 bytes with each byte containing 8 bits.

An easy way to create these graphics is to use BIN function which is short for Binary. The BIN function will covert a string of 1s and 0s into a decimal number.

Binary on the spectrum ranges from 0 to 255 which each 0 or 1 digit representing a number which doubles the value of the previous digit.

Digit 1	Digit 2	Digit 3	Digit 4	Digit 5	Digit 6	Digit 7	Digit 8
1 = 1	1 = 2	1 = 4	1 = 8	1 = 16	1 = 32	1 = 64	1 = 128

All 8 digits (working from right to left) would total to make 255. Below is an example of binary data to make a basic tree shape and the decimal equivalents of each bye of the UDG. A UDG contains 8 bytes of data. E.g. BIN 00000011 = 3

Here is an example of what Binary => Decimal looks like

```
              87654321
0 0 0 1 1 1 0 0   00011100        28
0 0 1 0 1 0 1 0   00101010        42
0 1 0 0 1 0 0 1   01001001        73
0 0 0 1 1 1 0 0   00011100        28
0 0 1 0 1 0 1 0   00101010        42
0 1 0 0 1 0 0 1   01001001        73
0 0 0 1 1 1 0 0   00011100        28
0 0 1 1 1 1 1 0   00111110        62
```

Tip: Using code to create UDGs is relatively easy, USR "a" is the first UDG character.

```
7010 FOR n = 0 TO 7
7020 READ graph
7030 POKE USR "a"+n,graph
7050 NEXT n
7060 RETURN
7200 DATA BIN 00111100, BIN 01100110, BIN 01011110, BIN
01011110, BIN 01111110, BIN 00111100, BIN 00000000, BIN
00000000
```

Suggestions for Extending (optional)

1] Add more level formations
2] Add power-ups

SNAKE BITE

> *You must help the snake survive and grow by eating the apples that are falling from the trees. Try to eat as many as possible without running into the side of the screen or your own tail! Good Luck! Myself and classroom buddies spent a lot of time playing this DOS game on our IBMs during our computer classes. It also appeared later on the Nokia phones and was one of the first original mobile phone games!*

Players:　1

Rules:　Player tries to eat as many apples as possible and beat their high score.

　Running into the borders or your own tail will end the game.

Controls:　q = up, a = down, o = left, p = right.

```
 10 REM ******ZX Spectrum Code Club *******
 15 REM * SNAKE BITE by Gary Plowman 2015 *
 20 REM ********************************
 25 LET hsc=0: GO SUB 6000:
 30 INK 1: PAPER 7: BORDER 4: CLS
 45 REM ****** Initialising variables
 50 PRINT AT 2,10; INK 7; BRIGHT 1; PAPER 2;"SNAKE BITE":
PRINT AT 4,5;"Control your snake *"
 35 LET lives=3
 60 PRINT AT 7,5;"Avoid your tail! *****"
 65 PRINT AT 8,5;"Eat the apples"; PAPER 6;"o"
 70 PRINT AT 11,2;"Controls: ";AT 12,2;"Q/A=Up/Down,
O/P=Left/Right"
 80 PRINT AT 18,5; FLASH 1;"PRESS A KEY TO START": PAUSE 0
100 GO SUB 300: REM initialise
```

```
 130 GO SUB 1000: REM main loop for game
 200 GO TO 30:
 300 REM *** SETUP
 310 LET x=10: LET y=10: LET vx=0: LET vy=0: LET score=0: LET
lvl=1: LET ax=1: LET ay=1: LET ax2=0: LET ay2=0: LET loot=0:
LET snk = 5: LET dx=x-5: LET dy=y: LET longer=0: LET snkpos=1:
LET ny=0: LET nx=0: LET ly=0: LET lx=0
 330 RETURN
1000 CLS
1010 FOR n = 0 TO 19:
1030 PRINT AT n,0;CHR$ (136);AT n,31;CHR$ (136)
1040 NEXT n
1045 FOR n=1 TO 30
1050 PRINT AT 0,n;CHR$ (136);AT 19,n;CHR$ (136)
1060 NEXT n
1087 PRINT AT INT (RND*15)+3,INT (RND*25)+3; PAPER 6;"o"
1095 PRINT AT 20,1;"Score: ";score
1096 FOR n=1 TO 5
1097 PRINT AT y,x-n;"*"
1098 NEXT n
1099 PRINT AT y,x;"*"
1100 LET i$=INKEY$: LET i=IN 31
1110 IF (i$="q" OR i=8) AND y>2 THEN LET vy=-1: LET vx=0
1120 IF (i$="a" OR i=4) AND y<19 THEN LET vy=1: LET vx=0
1130 IF (i$="o" OR i=1) AND x>2 THEN LET vx=-1: LET vy=0
1140 IF (i$="p" OR i=2) AND y<30 THEN LET vx=1: LET vy=0
1145 LET x=x+vx: LET y  =y+vy
1150 IF x=0 THEN GO SUB 2000
1160 IF x=31 THEN GO SUB 2000
1170 IF y=19 THEN GO SUB 2000
1180 IF y=0 THEN GO SUB 2000
1185 LET a$=SCREEN$ (y,x)
1200 IF a$="o" THEN GO SUB 3000
1210 IF vx<>0 OR vy<>0 THEN GO SUB 2500
1230 PRINT AT y,x;"*"
1300 GO TO 1100
```

```
1900 STOP
2000 PRINT AT 10,10;"DEAD!";AT 15,10; FLASH 1;"RESTARTING":
BEEP 2,1: PAUSE 1000
2010 IF score>hsc THEN LET hsc=score
2100 GO TO 30
2500 REM *** DRAW SNAKE
2510 IF a$="*" AND (vx<>0 OR vy<>0) THEN GO SUB 2000
2520 PRINT AT dy,dx;" ":
2525 IF longer>0 THEN LET longer=longer-1: RETURN
2526 LET mx=0: LET nx=0: LET ny=0
2530 IF SCREEN$ (dy-1,dx)="*" THEN LET ny=-1: LET mx=mx+1
2540 IF SCREEN$ (dy+1,dx)="*" THEN LET ny=1: LET mx=mx+1
2550 IF SCREEN$ (dy,dx-1)="*" THEN LET nx=-1: LET mx=mx+1
2560 IF SCREEN$ (dy,dx+1)="*" THEN LET nx=1: LET mx=mx+1
2570 IF mx>1 THEN GO SUB 4000
2575 LET dy = dy + ny: LET dx=dx+nx
2580 RETURN
3000 REM *** EAT APPLE
3010 LET score = score +(INT (RND*4)+1)
3020 PRINT AT 20,1; PAPER 1; INK 7;"Score: ";score;AT
20,16;"Hi-Score: ";hsc: BEEP .05,20
3030 LET ax=INT (RND*25)+3: LET ay=INT (RND*15)+3
3040 IF SCREEN$ (ay,ax)="*" THEN GO TO 3030
3050 PRINT AT ay,ax; PAPER 6;"o": BEEP .1,1: LET longer=2
3060 RETURN
4000 REM *** Follow correct route
4010 LET r1=0: LET r2=0
4020 IF SCREEN$ (dy+ny,dx)="*" THEN LET r1=r1+1
4030 IF SCREEN$ (dy+(ny*2),dx)="*" THEN LET r1=r1+1
4040 IF SCREEN$ (dy+(ny*3),dx)="*" THEN LET r1=r1+1
4050 IF SCREEN$ (dy,dx+nx)="*" THEN LET r2=r2+1
4060 IF SCREEN$ (dy,dx+(nx*2))="*" THEN LET r2=r2+1
4070 IF SCREEN$ (dy,dx+(nx*3))="*" THEN LET r2=r2+1
4075 IF r1>r2 THEN LET nx=0: LET ly=ny: LET lx=0: RETURN
4080 IF r1<r2 THEN LET ny=0: LET lx=nx: LET ly=0: RETURN
4090 IF r1=r2 THEN LET nx=lx: LET ny=ly
```

```
4095 PRINT AT 19,10;"R1=";r1;" R2=";r2
4100 RETURN
7000 FOR n = 0 TO 7
7010 READ dat
7020 POKE USR "a"+n,dat
7030 NEXT n
7040 RETURN
7050 DATA 16,60,66,218,75,66,60,8
```

What's New?

The main thing that is new here is a second method for controls. IN 31 is used to read the Joystick port of the machine (or emulator). So now you will have the ability to use joystick controls in your games. Yes, it's really that easy to add joystick controls to a Sinclair BASIC game. Lines 1100 to 1140 contain the code to detect both keyboard and joystick controls for your game. That's only 5 lines of code!

```
1100 LET i$=INKEY$: LET i=IN 31
1110 IF (i$="q" OR i=8) AND y>2 THEN LET vy=-1: LET vx=0
1120 IF (i$="a" OR i=4) AND y<19 THEN LET vy=1: LET vx=0
1130 IF (i$="o" OR i=1) AND x>2 THEN LET vx=-1: LET vy=0
1140 IF (i$="p" OR i=2) AND y<30 THEN LET vx=1: LET vy=0
```

To use one of more **Sinclair** joystick port options, you need only setup keys 1,2,3,4 and 5 or 6,7,8,9 and 0 these keys would be equivalent of left, right, down, up and fire.

Speed

In order to keep the game running at the same speed throughout, without resulting to any machine code, we used a custom tail eating routine for our snake. And to allow the snake to grow we delayed the tail eating routine each time the snake ate.

Collision Detection

Commands like SCREEN$ (dy+ny,dx)="*" can be useful for testing for collision or letting the program know where objects can move to, or if part of the screen is empty or not. Keep this in mind when you are creating any of your own games.

High Scoring

My personal best at this version of the game is 72. Try to beat that if you can!

IF x THEN y

All games need to perform decisions. These decisions in BASIC are performed using IF THEN statements. IF x=1 THEN do something : now do something else : and so on. IF statements in Sinclair BASIC are quite simple and execute only a single line of commands. They do not have the ELSE or ELSEIF alternative conditions. But you can branch off and perform multiple commands using a GOTO or a GO SUB. Throughout this book we will also see IF statements with multiple conditions to meet using the AND / OR Boolean expressions.

Simple Boolean expression example

Between the IF and THEN you can have a number of different expressions which you can test as TRUE or FALSE and you can combine and order those expressions using brackets and using the Boolean operators of AND and OR.

The AND expression returns TRUE if both sides are TRUE:

1 AND 1 = TRUE   1 AND 0 = FALSE

The OR expression returns TRUE if at least one side is TRUE:

1 OR 0 = TRUE   0 OR 0 = FALSE

With these added, your statement becomes something like this:

IF (a=x OR b=x) AND c=x THEN y

In the above line the bracketed expressions are first tested then their result is tested against the last expression using the AND operator.

Another Boolean operator you can use is NOT. This reverses the result of the expression that it is used with, so NOT 1=1 would equate as FALSE instead of TRUE and the expression NOT 1=0 would equate as TRUE.

Basic BEEP Sounds

The BEEP command is nice and simple. You have two settings BEEP duration, pitch. Here is a simple Piano scale for some of the BEEP values.

...	C	C#	D	D#	E	F	F#	G	G#	A	A#	B	C	...
←	0	1	2	3	4	5	6	7	8	9	10	11	12	→

Duration is measured in seconds or fractions of a second. i.e. .5 seconds

So for the musicians among you, try add some simple music to your games.

128k Mode offers another option in the form of the PLAY command that uses the more musical AY chip, but for easy of use and compatibility we will just be using BEEP.

Suggestions for Extending (optional)

1] *Add UDGs and use colour attributes for collision detections*
2] *Add more obstacles to avoid*
3] *Add timer to put more pressure on the player to act quickly*

FLAPPY BIRD

The world went Flappy mad in 2014. Flappy Bird was everywhere and with the news that the developer created the game in such a short time frame thousands of new coders came on the scene. It re-ignited an interest in bedroom-coding in many countries around the world. I created a version in BASIC that same year, just for fun. Its not as fast as the original but who cares! It's still Flappy Bird, especially if you increase the emulator speed. Enjoy!

Players: 1

Rules: Player tries to get through the oncoming pipes without crashing into them.
              Player tries to beat their high score.

Controls: Press any key to stay in the air. That's it!

```
   1 REM Speccy Conversion by G Plowman ( Gazzapper Games)
   2 PRINT AT 10,10;"LOADING GRAPHICS"
   3 GO SUB 3000
   5 BRIGHT 1
   6 PAPER 7
   7 INK 1: CLS
   8 LET hscore=0
  10 PRINT AT 1,0: INK 2: PRINT "=== =    ==== ==== ==== =
="
  20 INK 3: PRINT "=    =    = = =   = =   = =  ="
  21 INK 4: PRINT "=== =    ==== ==== ==== ===="
  22 INK 5: PRINT "=    =    = = =     =      ="
  24 INK 1: PRINT "=    =    = = =     =      ="
  26 INK 3: PRINT "=    =    = = =     =      ="
  28 INK 2: PRINT "=    === = = =     =      ="
```

```
 30 PRINT ""
 32 INK 4: PRINT "====  == ==== ==="
 34 INK 2: PRINT "=  =  == =  = =   ="
 36 INK 1: PRINT "====  == ==== =   ="
 38 INK 4: PRINT "=  =  == = =  =   ="
 40 INK 3: PRINT "=  =  == =  = =   ="
 42 INK 5: PRINT "====  == =  = ==="
 43 PRINT "": INK 0
 48 PRINT "SINCLAIR SPECTRUM CONVERSION"
 49 PRINT "By Gary Plowman- Orig .Gears"
 50 PRINT
 51 PRINT " PRESS A KEY TO START"
 53 PRINT " (CONTROLS : ANY KEY TO FLY"
 55 LET b$=""   : LET c$=""
 56 FOR n=1 TO 30: LET b$=b$+CHR$ (132): LET c$=c$+CHR$ (136)
: NEXT n
 58 INK 3: PRINT AT 19,0;b$
 60 FOR n=1 TO 30
 62 PRINT AT 1,n;" ";CHR$ (144)
 64 PAUSE 5
 66 PRINT AT 1,n;" ";CHR$ (145)
 68 BEEP .02,1
 70 PAUSE 5
 75 IF INKEY$<>"" THEN GO TO 200
 80 NEXT n
 85 PRINT AT 1,n;"  ":
 86 GO TO 60
200 LET score=INT (0): LET r=1
202 DIM x(10): DIM h(10)
203 LET pipes=1
204 LET fly=12: LET anim=0
205 BRIGHT 1: PAPER 7: INK 2
206 CLS
210 PRINT AT 10,10;"G E T  R E A D Y!"
220 PRINT ""
```

```
222 INK 1: PRINT AT 12,10;"   ";CHR$ (144)
226 PRINT
227 INK 2: PRINT "       Tap To Fly"
230 IF INKEY$="" THEN GO TO 230
300 REM ****** START **********
302 FOR o=1 TO 10
303 LET h(o)=INT (RND*8)+1
305 NEXT o
306 FOR l=1 TO 10
308 LET x(l)=25+(l*5)
309 NEXT l
310 GO SUB 1000
600 GO TO 310
999 REM **********************
1000 REM **** DRAW PIPES
1002 CLS
1010 INK 1: PRINT AT fly,10;"   ";CHR$ (144): LET fly=fly+1
1011 INK 3: PLOT 0,20: DRAW 240,0
1012 IF anim=1 THEN INK 1: PRINT AT fly-1,10;"   ";CHR$ (145)
1013 LET anim=0
1016 LET r=r+1
1017 INK 3: PRINT AT 0,2;"SCORE: ";score: PRINT AT 0,20;"HI-
SCORE:";hscore
1018 IF INKEY$<>"" THEN LET fly=fly-2: BEEP .01,2
1030 FOR p=1 TO 10
1033 IF INKEY$<>"" THEN LET anim=1
1035 INK 4
1039 LET bh=h(p)*8: IF x(p)<30 AND x(p)>1 AND h(p)>0 THEN PLOT
x(p)*8,3*8: DRAW 0,bh: DRAW 8,0: DRAW 0,-(bh)
1040 LET nh=INT ((13-(h(p)))*8): IF x(p)<30 AND x(p)>1 AND
h(p)>0 THEN PLOT x(p)*8,150: DRAW 0,-nh: DRAW 8,0: DRAW 0,nh
1041 IF x(p)<1 THEN LET h(p)=INT (RND*8)+1
1042 IF x(p)<1 THEN LET x(p)=40
1050 REM INK 3: IF p=4 THEN PRINT AT 19,0;c$
1052 LET x(p)=x(p)-1
1059 IF x(p)=9 AND h(p)>0 THEN BEEP .02,3: LET score=score+1
```

```
1070 IF x(p)=12 AND fly>19-h(p) THEN GO SUB 1200
1075 IF x(p)=12 AND fly<19-(h(p)+3) THEN GO SUB 1200
1076 IF fly=20 THEN GO SUB 1200
1080 NEXT p
1100 RETURN
1200 REM **** DEAD ****
1210 PRINT AT 10,4;"OUCH!!"
1220 BEEP .3,7: BEEP .3,2: BEEP .5,-3
1240 PRINT AT 12,4;"HIT ENTER TO RESTART!"
1300 IF INKEY$=CHR$ (13) THEN GO TO 200
1310 GO TO 1300
3000 LET daa=0
3002 FOR n=0 TO 167
3005 READ DAA
3010 DATA
12,18,37,193,254,66,60,0,12,18,37,193,254,126,0,0,0,60,66,64,6
4,66,60,0,0,120,68,66,66,68,120,0,0,126,64,124,64,64,126,0,0,1
26,64,124,64,64,64,0,0,60,66,64,78,66,60,0,0,66,66,126,66,66,6
6,0,0,62,8,8,8,8,62,0,0,2,2,2,66,66,60,0,0,68,72,112,72,68,66,
0,0,64,64,64,64,64,126,0,0,66,102,90,66,66,66,0,0,66,98,82,74,
70,66,0,0,60,66,66,66,66,60,0,0,124,66,66,124,64,64,0,0,60,66,
66,82,74,60,0,0,124,66,66,124,68,66,0,0,60,64,60,2,66,60,0,0,2
54,16,16,16,16,16,0,0,66,66,66,66,66,60,0,0
3030 POKE USR "a"+n,daa
3040 NEXT n
3050 RETURN
```

What's New?

So now that you have typed in a Spectrum version of Flappy Bird you can see how such a fun game can be done with simple code. Okay, maybe parts of the code here are a little confusing to you but that is probably down to the use of maths. It is quite easy once explained, the screen collision detection for pipes were multiplied out by 8 to allow for the pipes to be drawn on the pixel screen grid of 256 (x-axis) by 192 (y-axis) pixels. But the actual collision detection was based on the character printing grid of 32 (x-axis) by 22 (y-axis) character positions. Just so it is easier to understand, when comparing character printing locations to pixel locations we need to multiply or divide by a factor of 8. For every 8 pixels there is 1 character position. See the diagram below on how the screen work for pixels and characters.

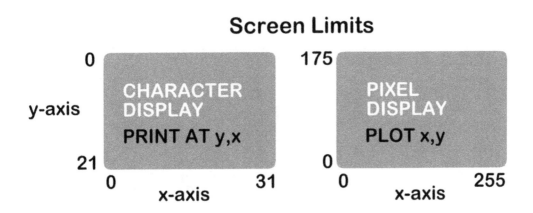

Hello Colour Clash

A known limitation of the Sinclair Spectrum is that only two colours can exist within each character position on the screen (8 x 8 pixels). This adds a bit of retro-charm to the games when they clash together. You will notice this feature in this game as your Flappy Bird collides with the pipes. There you go, that's colour clash!

Basic Animation

Animating with UDGs (a.k.a. Sprites) is executed very simply here.

```
1033 IF INKEY$<>"" THEN LET anim=1
```

The line above sets the anim value to 1 so that we can know to draw the flapping bird UDG sprite, thus making our bird flap his wings.

```
1012 IF anim=1 THEN INK 1: PRINT AT fly-1,10;"  ";CHR$ (145)
```

This is a very simple method but easily done, to do more than one frame of animation usually involves tracking movement with a timer value. But that level of detail is for another time. The first part of the PRINT command clears the old position of our bird before printing at the new position.

```
302 FOR o=1 TO 10
303 LET h(o)=INT (RND*8)+1
305 NEXT o
306 FOR l=1 TO 10
308 LET x(l)=25+(l*5)
309 NEXT l
```

Above creates our pipe positions and heights but will not display them until they have scrolled left enough to show on our screen.

Suggestions for Extending (optional)

1]   *Add enemies*
2]   *Remove the top pipes and work on a Scramble clone!*

THE NUMBERS GAME

> *I love "8 Out of 10 Cats Does Countdown" and I love trying to solve the Math bits! This is inspired by that. It's not terribly advanced but give it a go and see if you can solve your own problems! Maybe you might be inspired to create the 'words' version at a later date?*

Players: 1

Rules: Player tries to calculate the result using the numbers provided and maths commands.

Controls: Typing in the respective values and commands: 'add', 'mult' and 'sub'.

```
  10 REM *********ZX CODE CLUB****************
  15 REM * The Numbers Game (Countdown)        *
  20 REM ***********G.Plowman*****************
  30 INK 0: PAPER 5: BORDER 4: CLS
  45 REM ****** Initialising variables
  50 PRINT AT 2,7; INK 7; BRIGHT 1; PAPER 7; INK 3;"The
Numbers Game": PRINT AT 4,5;""
  60 PRINT AT 4,5;"Mathletes Get Ready!"
  80 PRINT AT 18,5; FLASH 1;"PRESS A KEY TO START": PAUSE 0:
CLS
 100 REM GO SUB 5000: REM Graphics
 110 GO SUB 300: REM initialise:
 130 GO SUB 1000: REM draw screen
 140 GO SUB 2000: main loop
 300 REM **** init
 310 LET p1=0: LET p2=0: LET p3=0: LET p4=0: LET p5=0: LET
p$="": LET q$="": LET r$="":
```

```
 320 LET s$="": LET t$="":
 330 RETURN
1000 REM ****** Screen
1005 PRINT AT 3,10; PAPER 7; BRIGHT 1; INK 3;"THE NUMBERS
GAME"
1010 FOR n=5 TO 10
1020 PRINT AT n,10; PAPER 7;"                    "
1030 NEXT n
1040 PRINT AT 5,3; INK 6;CHR$ (137);CHR$ (143);CHR$ (143);CHR$
(143);CHR$ (134)
1060 PRINT AT 6,2; INK 6;CHR$ (133); PAPER 7; CHR$ (138);CHR$
(137);" ";CHR$ (137); INK 6;CHR$ (133); PAPER 5;CHR$ (138)
1070 PRINT AT 7,2; INK 6;CHR$ (133); PAPER 7;CHR$ (138); INK
1;CHR$ (132);" ";CHR$ (132); INK 6;CHR$ (133); PAPER 5;CHR$
(138)
1080 PRINT AT 8,2; INK 6;CHR$ (133); PAPER 7;CHR$ (138);"   ";
PAPER 5;CHR$ (143)
1090 PRINT AT 9,2; INK 6;CHR$ (133); PAPER 7;CHR$ (138); INK
2;CHR$ (132);CHR$ (140);" "; INK 6; PAPER 5;CHR$ (143)
1100 PRINT AT 10,3; INK 6;CHR$ (133); PAPER 7;CHR$ (138);" ";
INK 6;CHR$ (133)
1110 PRINT AT 11,4; PAPER 7;"   "
1200 FOR n = 12 TO 18
1205 RANDOMIZE
1210 LET c=INT (RND*4)+3
1215 PRINT AT n+1,3; INK INT (RND*4);CHR$ (143);CHR$
(143);CHR$ (143);AT n,4;CHR$ (143);CHR$ (143);;AT n+1,5;CHR$
(143);CHR$ (143)
1230 NEXT n
1250 FOR n=13 TO 19 STEP 2
1260 PRINT AT n,14; PAPER 7;"  "; PAPER 5;" "; PAPER 7;"  ";
PAPER 5;" "; PAPER 7;"  "; PAPER 5;" "; PAPER 7;"  "
1270 NEXT n
2000 PRINT AT 1,10;"PRESS S TO START"
2010 LET i$=INKEY$
2020 IF i$="s" THEN GO TO 2100
```

```
2030 GO TO 2010
2100 RANDOMIZE
2105 LET ans=0: LET ans1=0
2110 LET n1=INT (RND*90)+10
2120 LET n2=INT (RND*10)+2
2130 LET n3=INT (RND*10)+2
2140 LET n4=INT (RND*10)+2
2150 LET n5=INT (RND*10)+2
2170 LET o1=INT (RND*4)+1
2180 LET o2=INT (RND*4)+1
2190 LET o3=INT (RND*4)+1
2195 LET o4=INT (RND*4)+1:
2200 PRINT PAPER 1; INK 7;AT 8,12;n1; PAPER 7;" "; PAPER 1;n2;
PAPER 7;" "; PAPER 1;n3; PAPER 7;" "; PAPER 1;n4; PAPER 7;" ";
PAPER 1;n5; PAPER 7;" ":
2210 IF o1=1 THEN LET ans=n1-n2
2220 IF o1=2 THEN LET ans=n1*n2
2230 IF o1>2 THEN LET ans=n1+n2
2240 IF o2=1 AND n3>n4 THEN LET ans1=n3-n4
2245 IF o2=1 AND n3<n4 THEN LET ans1=n4-n3
2250 IF o2=2 THEN LET ans1=n3*n4
2260 IF o2>2 THEN LET ans1=n3-n4:
2270 IF o3=1 THEN LET ans=ans+ans1-n5
2280 IF o3=2 THEN LET ans=ans*n5+ans1
2290 IF o3>2 THEN LET ans=ans+ans1+n5
2295 IF ans<100 THEN GO TO 2100:
2300 PRINT AT 6,12;ans
2310 INPUT "Enter a number from the cards above:",p1
2315 IF p1<>n1 AND p1<>n2 AND p1<>n3 AND p1<>n4 AND p1<>n5
THEN BEEP .5,0: PRINT AT 11,10;"WRONG NUMBER": GO TO 2310
2320 INPUT "Enter command add,sub or mult:", LINE p$
2330 INPUT "Enter next number from the cards above:",p2
2335 IF p2<>n1 AND p2<>n2 AND p2<>n3 AND p2<>n4 AND p2<>n5
THEN BEEP .5,0: PRINT AT 11,10;"WRONG NUMBER": GO TO 2330
2340 INPUT "Enter command add, sub, mult or calc:", LINE q$
2345 IF q$="calc" THEN GO SUB 3000
```

```
2350 INPUT "Enter next number from the cards above:",p3
2355 IF p3<>n1 AND p3<>n2 AND p3<>n3 AND p3<>n4 AND p3<>n5
THEN BEEP .5,0: PRINT AT 11,10;"WRONG NUMBER": GO TO 2350
2360 INPUT "Enter command add, sub, mult or calc:", LINE r$
2370 IF r$="calc" THEN GO SUB 3000
2380 INPUT "Enter next number from the cards above:",p4
2385 IF p4<>n1 AND p4<>n2 AND p4<>n3 AND p4<>n4 AND p4<>n5
THEN BEEP .5,0: PRINT AT 11,10;"WRONG NUMBER": GO TO 2380
2390 INPUT "Enter command add, sub, mult or calc:", LINE s$
2400 IF s$="calc" THEN GO SUB 3000
2410 INPUT "Enter next number from the cards above:",p5
2420 IF p5<>n1 AND p5<>n2 AND p5<>n3 AND p5<>n4 AND p5<>n5
THEN BEEP .5,0: PRINT AT 11,10;"WRONG NUMBER": GO TO 2380:
2440 IF p$="calc" THEN GO SUB 3000:
2490 GO SUB 3000
3000 REM ***** CHECK ANSWER
3010 LET answer=0
3020 IF p$="add" THEN LET answer = p1+p2
3030 IF p$="sub" THEN LET answer = p1-p2
3040 IF p$="mult" THEN LET answer= p1*p2
3050 IF q$="add" THEN LET answer = answer+ p3
3060 IF q$="sub" THEN LET answer = answer-p3
3070 IF q$="mult" THEN LET answer= answer*p3
3080 IF r$="add" THEN LET answer = answer+p4
3090 IF r$="sub" THEN LET answer = answer-p4
3100 IF r$="mult" THEN LET answer= answer*p4
3110 IF s$="add" THEN LET answer = answer+p5
3120 IF s$="sub" THEN LET answer = answer-p5
3130 IF s$="mult" THEN LET answer= answer*p5
3200 IF answer = ans THEN BEEP 1,6: PRINT AT 11,10; INK
1;"Yay! ";answer;" is correct!"
3210 IF answer<>ans THEN BEEP 1,-7: PRINT AT 11,10; INK 2;"You
Got ";answer;"    "
3250 PRINT AT 12,10;"Press to Play Again": PAUSE 0
3260 GO TO 1000
```

Progress

Well how are you getting along with BASIC? You should be understanding what certain commands are specifically used for by now. You will have noticed a lot of Character codes in the last listing. These can be looked up at the end of the book in Appendix A.

Input

We used a fair amount of INPUT commands. This is quite a useful command for asking the user to perform actions or make decisions. It is very useful for text adventure games or interactive stories where the users decisions can change the route of the story.

PEEKs and POKEs

For our UDG graphics we used a command called POKE. This commands places a decimal value into a memory location. We then can collect this value again using a PEEK command.

e.g. Try POKE 33000,45 then enter, now try PEEK 33000 to get the value back.

Maths Functions

Sinclair BASIC has a lot of maths functions. It is not perfect, nor does it have every function but it has the majority of what a beginner would need for simple Trigonometry or Algebra. Examples: PI (that 3.141592…etc.), EXP (Exponential), LN (Logarithms), SIN (Sine), COS (Cosine), TAN (Tangent).

Suggestions for Extending (optional)

1]   *Add more complex math solutions*
2]   *Add the letter / words part of the Countdown game*

BATTLESHIP WAR

Another classic Pen and Paper game. Battleship War is the computerized version of the game with some small amendments. Pick your grid to place your ships. Make sure your opponent is not looking to see where you are placing. Then when your finished it's their turn to put there ships on the grid. The winner is player that destroys all their opponents ships. So get typing and get playing!

Players: 2

Rules: Place your ships on the grid by pressing in the keys for the coordinates. The winner is the player who destroys all the opponents ships.

Controls: Keys A to J for horizontal and 1 to 9 for vertical placement on the grid or firing shots. R to rotate the ship position before hitting ENTER to save.

Tip: A nice big piece of cardboard is good for hiding screens during 'hotseat' play.

```
 10 REM ****** ZX Code Club **************
 15 REM * BATTLESHIP WAR by Gary Plowman  *
 20 REM *********************************
 30 INK 7: PAPER 0: BORDER 4: CLS
 40 PRINT AT 5,10; INK 2;"BATTLESHIP WAR"
 50 PRINT AT 10,5;"2 Player Game (hotseat)"
 60 PRINT AT 12,5; BRIGHT 1; INVERSE 1;"1. Start Game"
 70 PRINT AT 15,2;"Use a card to hide some"
 80 PRINT AT 16,2;"of the screen or look away"
 90 PRINT AT 17,2;"when other player is placing";AT
18,2;"their units":
100 IF INKEY$="1" THEN LET gm=1: GO TO 130
120 GO TO 100
```

```
130 BEEP .2,7: BEEP .6,2: BEEP .3,-3: BEEP .7,9
135 INPUT "ENTER # SHIPS EACH (2 to 5):";noships
140 BORDER 5: CLS
150 PRINT AT 1,10; INK 2;"BATTLESHIP WAR":
160 GO SUB 190
170 GO TO 270
180 REM ********************** Redo Board *
190 FOR n=6 TO 14
200 PRINT AT n,5; PAPER 5; INK 1;"----------"
210 PRINT AT n,17; PAPER 5; INK 1;"----------"
220 PRINT AT n,3; PAPER 3;n-5;AT n,28;n-5
230 NEXT n
240 LET a$="ABCDEFGHIJ"
250 PRINT AT 5,5;a$;AT 5,17;a$
260 RETURN
270 IF gm=2 THEN PRINT AT 18,3;"PLAYER 1 GET READY";AT
19,3;"PLAYER 2 LOOK AWAY"
280 PRINT AT 21,5; FLASH 1;"PRESS KEY TO CONTINUE"
290 IF INKEY$="" THEN GO TO 290
300 GO SUB 320
310 GO SUB 380
320 REM *************** Clearing part of screen
325 PRINT AT 17,0;"                              "
330 PRINT AT 18,0;"                              "
340 PRINT AT 19,0;"                              "
350 PRINT AT 20,0;"                              "
360 PRINT AT 21,0;"                              "
370 RETURN
380 REM *************** PLACING PLAYER 1 UNITS
390 DIM a(noships,2,2): DIM h(2): DIM f(2): DIM x(noships,2):
DIM y(5): LET shp1=1: LET shp2=1: LET r=0: LET m$="": LET
ply=1
400 PRINT AT 17,3;"Press Coords for ship ";shp1;AT 18,3;"e.g.
A5"
410 LET i$=INKEY$
```

```
 420 IF i$>="a" AND i$<="k" THEN LET a(shp1,1,ply)=(CODE
(i$))-96: LET m$=i$+STR$ (a(shp1,2,ply)): BEEP .05,6
 430 IF i$>="1" AND i$<="9" THEN LET a(shp1,2,ply)=VAL (i$):
LET m$=i$+STR$ (a(shp1,2,ply)): BEEP .05,7
 435 IF a(shp1,1,ply)=0 OR a(shp1,2,ply)=0 THEN GO TO 400
 440 IF ply=1 THEN PRINT AT 4,2;CHR$
(a(shp1,1,ply)+96);a(shp1,2,ply); INK 6;"  Ship# ";shp1
 445 IF ply=2 THEN PRINT AT 4,2;"            ";AT 4,17;CHR$
(a(shp1,1,ply)+96);a(shp1,2,ply); INK 6;"  Ship# ";shp1
 450 IF r=1 AND a(shp1,2,ply)>7 THEN LET r=NOT r
 460 IF i$="r" THEN LET r=NOT r
 470 IF r=0 AND a(shp1,1,ply)>7 THEN LET r=NOT r
 480 IF i$=CHR$ (13) AND a(shp1,2,ply)>0 AND a(shp1,1,ply)>0
THEN BEEP .3,2: LET shp1=shp1+1: GO SUB 320: REM ***********
clean part of screen / next unit
 490 IF shp1=noships+1 AND ply=1 THEN BEEP 1,7: BEEP .2,4: LET
shp1=1: LET ply=2: GO SUB 190
 500 IF shp1=noships+1 AND ply=2 THEN LET ply=1: BEEP 1,7:
BEEP .2,4: GO TO 1000
 505 IF a(shp1,2,ply)>0 AND a(shp1,1,ply)>0 THEN PRINT AT
20,0; INK 6;"[R] Rotate Ship";AT 21,0; FLASH 1;"[Enter] Next
Ship"
 510 IF a(shp1,1,ply)=0 OR a(shp1,2,ply)=0 THEN GO TO 400
 520 IF i$<>"" THEN GO SUB 190: REM *************** redo board
again *
 530 IF r=0 THEN LET x(shp1,ply)=0
 540 IF r=1 THEN LET x(shp1,ply)=1
 550 FOR n=1 TO shp1
 560 IF x(n,ply)=0 AND ply=1 THEN PRINT AT
a(n,2,ply)+5,a(n,1,ply)+4;"***"
 570 IF x(n,ply)=1 AND ply=1 THEN PRINT AT
a(n,2,ply)+5,a(n,1,ply)+4;"*";AT
a(n,2,ply)+6,a(n,1,ply)+4;"*";AT a(n,2,ply)+7,a(n,1,ply)+4;"*"
 580 IF x(n,ply)=0 AND ply=2 THEN PRINT AT
a(n,2,ply)+5,a(n,1,ply)+16;"***"
```

```
 590 IF x(n,ply)=1 AND ply=2 THEN PRINT AT
a(n,2,ply)+5,a(n,1,ply)+16;"*";AT
a(n,2,ply)+6,a(n,1,ply)+16;"*";AT
a(n,2,ply)+7,a(n,1,ply)+16;"*"
 600 NEXT n
 700 GO TO 400
1000 REM ***** TAKE TURNS
1005 LET hits=1: LET ply=1: LET hits1=1: LET hits2=1
1010 PRINT AT 4,2;"                        "
1020 GO SUB 190
1030 GO SUB 320
1040 PRINT AT 17,0;"PLAYER ";ply;"....FIRE SHOT..e.g. A5"
1050 GO SUB 2000: REM Get shot
2000 REM ****** Get Shot coords
2005 LET ply=ply+1
2006 IF ply>2 THEN LET ply=1
2008 PRINT AT 18,0;"Current Hits on Target: ";f(ply)
2010 LET i$=INKEY$
2020 IF i$>="a" AND i$<="k" THEN LET h(1)=(CODE (i$))-96: LET
m$=i$+STR$ (h(1)): BEEP .05,6
2030 IF i$>="1" AND i$<="9" THEN LET h(2)=VAL (i$): LET
m$=i$+STR$ (h(2)): BEEP .05,7
2040 IF h(1)>0 AND h(2)>0 THEN PRINT AT 20,0; INK
6;"FIRING...";h(1);"-";h(2): GO SUB 2300: GO TO 1030: REM ****
Check for hits
2050 IF f(ply)=noships*3 THEN GO SUB 2200:
2100 GO TO 2010
2200 REM ***** WINNER!
2210 PRINT AT 10,10;"PLAYER ";ply;" WINS!"
2220 FOR n = 1 TO 10
2230 BEEP .1,n+RND*2
2240 NEXT n
2250 BEEP 1,2: PAUSE 0
2260 GO TO 30
2260 RETURN
2300 REM **** Hit checks **************************
```

```
2305 LET miss=1
2316 IF ply=1 AND ATTR (h(2)+5,h(1)+4)<>41 THEN BEEP .1,-2: GO
TO 2380
2317 IF ply=2 AND ATTR (h(2)+5,h(1)+16)<>41 THEN BEEP .1,-2:
GO TO 2380
2320 FOR n=1 TO noships
2330 IF h(1)=a(n,1,ply) AND h(2)=a(n,2,ply) THEN LET miss=0:
LET f(ply)=f(ply)+1
2345 IF x(n,ply)=0 AND (h(1)-1=a(n,1,ply) OR h(1)-
2=a(n,1,ply)) AND h(2)=a(n,2,ply) THEN LET miss=0: LET
f(ply)=f(ply)+1
2346 IF x(n,ply)=1 AND (h(2)-1=a(n,2,ply) OR h(2)-
2=a(n,2,ply)) AND h(1)=a(n,1,ply) THEN LET miss=0: LET
f(ply)=f(ply)+1
2350 NEXT n
2360 IF ply=1 AND miss=0 THEN PRINT AT 21,0; FLASH 1;"PLAYER 2
SHIP HIT!";AT h(2)+5,h(1)+4; PAPER 2;"*"
2370 IF ply=2 AND miss=0 THEN PRINT AT 21,0; FLASH 1;"PLAYER 1
SHIP HIT!";AT h(2)+5,h(1)+16; PAPER 2;"*"
2380 IF miss=1 AND ply=2 AND ATTR (h(2)+5,h(1)+16)=41 THEN
PRINT AT 21,0;"YOU MISSED:!                ";AT h(2)+5,h(1)+16;
INK 6;"+": BEEP .3,7
2390 IF miss=1 AND ply=1 AND ATTR (h(2)+5,h(1)+4)=41 THEN
PRINT AT 21,0;"YOU MISSED!:                ";AT h(2)+5,h(1)+4;
INK 6;"+": BEEP .3,2
2400 LET h(1)=0: LET h(2)=0
2410 RETURN
```

What's New?

A lot more Array commands used here to keep status and locations of the ships. Don't worry if the array side of the code is confusing to you. Beginners mostly use arrays sparsely until they get a bit more confident, then they experiment with them.

For efficiency some parts of the screen may not need to be redrawn so we can avoid that by using selective clearing of the screen area after an action has occurred. Simple tricks like this help speed up your programs.

```
320 REM ************** Clearing part of screen
325 PRINT AT 17,0;"                              "
330 PRINT AT 18,0;"                              "
340 PRINT AT 19,0;"                              "
350 PRINT AT 20,0;"                              "
360 PRINT AT 21,0;"                              "
```

```
DIM a(noships,2,2)
```

The above array used as a storage container for ships (x ships), location (2 values x and y), player (2 players).

Also the commands CODE and STR$ are used for getting get key press values as grid coordinates. We then use m$ to display the selected coordinate.

```
2020 IF i$>="a" AND i$<="k" THEN LET h(1)=(CODE (i$))-96: LET
m$=i$+STR$ (h(1))
```

The array pointer is used to plot the ship position and rotation which is saved into the x(#,#) array. No need to worry if the arrays are confusing to you. With enough practice you will start to use them in your own code without any problems.

Suggestions for Extending (optional)

1]   Add CPU player options
2]   Add UDG graphics for the ships

CODEBREAK

It's WWII and the enemy is sending secret orders to their troops. You must crack the code to decrypt the messages! Okay, remember a little electronic game where you had to solve the colour code? Also there was a 2 player board game called MasterMind that worked using a second player to set the code and tell you if you worked out any of the sequence correctly.

Players: 1 or more (co-operative)

Rules: Limited turns to guess the colour code sequence. Choosing from Red, Blue, Green, Cyan, Magenta (purple) and Yellow. The CPU will tell you indicate Y with number of colours correct and in sequence and C for number of colours correct.

Controls: Enter a colour sequence per turn using previous turns to work out the code.

```
 10 REM ******ZX Spectrum Code Club *******
 15 REM * CODEBREAK by G Plowman 2015      *
 20 REM *********************************
 30 INK 1: PAPER 7: BORDER 4: CLS
 35 REM POKE 23617,128: REM **** PUT CURSOR IN CAPS MODE
 45 REM ****** Initialising variables
 50 PRINT AT 2,10; INK 7; BRIGHT 1; PAPER 2;"CODEBREAK":
PRINT AT 4,5;"Find the Colour Code!":
 60 PRINT AT 7,5;"Get code in sequence"
 70 PRINT AT 8,5;"Enter Colours 1 at a time.":
 80 PRINT AT 18,5; FLASH 1;"PRESS A KEY TO START": PAUSE 0
100 GO SUB 300: REM initialise
130 GO SUB 1000: REM main loop for game
```

```
 200 GO TO 30:
 300 REM ***** SETUP
 310 LET turn=1: DIM c(4): DIM t(4): DIM a$(1,1): LET col=0:
LET colseq=0: LET codeseq=1
 330 RETURN
1000 PAPER 4: CLS
1010 RANDOMIZE
1020 FOR n = 1 TO 4
1030 LET c(n)=INT (RND*5)+1
1040 NEXT n:
1050 GO SUB 2000: REM **** CREATE BOARD:
1100 REM **** START GAME LOOP
1005 PRINT AT 0,4;"C o d e   B r e a k "
1110 PRINT AT 2,2;"Turn:";turn;AT 20,0;"Seq:";codeseq
1120 PRINT AT 18,0;"Enter each letter for code"
1130 INPUT "Enter either r,g,b,c,m,y",a$(1,1):
1140 IF a$(1,1)="r" THEN LET t(codeseq)=2
1150 IF a$(1,1)="b" THEN LET t(codeseq)=1
1160 IF a$(1,1)="g" THEN LET t(codeseq)=4
1170 IF a$(1,1)="y" THEN LET t(codeseq)=6
1180 IF a$(1,1)="m" THEN LET t(codeseq)=3
1190 IF a$(1,1)="c" THEN LET t(codeseq)=5
1390 LET codeseq=codeseq+1
1400 IF codeseq=5 THEN LET codeseq=1: GO SUB 4000: REM ***
check CODE
1900 GO TO 1100:
2000 FOR n = 1 TO 15
2010 PRINT AT 2+n,10; PAPER 7; BRIGHT 1;"[      ]"; PAPER 5;"
"; PAPER 6;"      "
2020 NEXT n
2030 REM FOR n = 1 TO 4: PRINT AT 2,10+n; INK c(n);CHR$ (143)
2040 REM NEXT n: rem **** Un-REM if you want to see code
2050 RETURN
4000 REM checking code value
4010 LET col=0: LET colseq=0
4020 FOR n = 1 TO 4
```

```
4030 IF t(n)=c(n) THEN LET colseq=colseq+1: GO TO 4050
4040 IF t(n)<>c(n) AND (t(n)=c(1) OR t(n)=c(2) OR t(n)=c(3) OR
t(n)=c(4)) THEN LET col=col+1
4050 NEXT n
4060 LET turn=turn+1
4070 PRINT AT   18-turn,18; PAPER 7;"Y=";colseq;" C=";col
4080 FOR n = 1 TO 4: PRINT AT 18-turn,10+n; PAPER t(n);" ":
NEXT n
4090 IF turn=15 THEN PRINT AT 10,10;" YOU LOSE ": GO SUB 4300:
4100 IF colseq=4 THEN PRINT AT 10,5;"CONGRATS CODEBREAKER!";AT
12,5;"PRESS TO PLAY AGAIN": PAUSE 0: GO TO 30
4110 RETURN
4300 REM Lost
4310 PRINT PAPER 7;AT 12,10;"              ";AT 13,10;"
";AT 14,10;"              "
4320 FOR n = 1 TO 4
4340 PRINT AT 13,12+n; PAPER c(n);" "
4350 NEXT n
4360 PAUSE 0
4370 GO TO 30
```

Simple but fun

It's a simple colourful game that one of more players can play. Players can debate and agree on the colours to use in the sequence. Lines 2030 and 2040 allow for a little cheat mode for testing your program is working correctly. To use you would need to remove the REM at the start of each line.

What's New?

RANDOMIZE is used to generate a new Random Seed value. When placed after user responses this makes your program much more random when using RND functions. Another use was found here for our friend the Array. However it is a more simple and straightforward usage this time.

```
1180 IF a$(1,1)="m" THEN LET t(codeseq)=3
```

The array t() is used to save our code sequence as a numeric value for each colour. We then check those to let the user know how they are getting on with **colseq** counting exact colour and sequence matches, and **col** value just counting correct colours present.

```
4000 REM checking code value
4010 LET col=0: LET colseq=0
4020 FOR n = 1 TO 4
4030 IF t(n)=c(n) THEN LET colseq=colseq+1: GO TO 4050
4040 IF t(n)<>c(n) AND (t(n)=c(1) OR t(n)=c(2) OR t(n)=c(3) OR
t(n)=c(4)) THEN LET col=col+1
4050 NEXT n
```

A note on Debugging

It is good practice to use PRINT and other commands to show you key information when Debugging your programs. Also another very useful command is the STOP command. You can use this with an IF statement to search and test for certain conditions that you want to avoid or fix. STOP will simply end the program at that line and return the user to the BASIC prompt.

Suggestions for Extending (optional)

1] Add more colour and graphics to the game in general
*2] Add a 2 player option where the one player can choose the
    code*

ASTRAL INVADERS

Prepare to defend your base! The Aliens are attacking! How long can you survive the onslaught of the oncoming aliens who are here to enslave your people. The Space Invaders theme never gets old and nearly everyone has enjoyed a version of this classic 80s game. The game is fun and addictive with nice colourful UDG graphics, so get coding and start zapping some aliens.

Players: 1

Rules: Space Invader / Galaxian-type game that is reminiscent of those table-top electronic games like Astro Wars etc. Shoot the aliens before they attack your base. Letting them get past will result in losing a life. Good fun!

Controls: z = left, x = right, [space]=fire.

```
  10 REM ******ZX Spectrum Code Club *******
  15 REM * ASTRAL INVADERS by Gary Plowman *
  20 REM *************2015******************
  30 INK 7: PAPER 0: BORDER 0: CLS
  45 REM ****** Initialising variables
  50 PRINT AT 2,8; INK 7; BRIGHT 1; PAPER 0;"ASTRAL INVADERS":
PRINT AT 4,6;"DONT LET THEM LAND";AT 6,1; INK 6;"Controls:";AT
8,1;"Z=Left, X=Right, Space to fire"
  80 PRINT AT 18,5; FLASH 1;"PRESS A KEY TO START": PAUSE 0:
LET hisc=0
 100 GO SUB 5000: REM Graphics
 110 GO SUB 300: REM initialise
 130 GO SUB 1000: REM main loop for game
 200 GO TO 30
 300 REM ***** SETUP
```

```
 310 LET lives=5: LET score=0: LET lvl=1: LET ax=INT
(RND*16)+6: LET ay=1: LET alien=145+INT (RND*3): LET acol=INT
(RND*6)+1: LET x=10: LET l$="L E V E L   O N E"
 315 LET speed=.1
 320 RESTORE 340
 305 RANDOMIZE
 390 RETURN
1000 CLS : PRINT AT 0,7;l$: REM ******* MAIN GAME
1010 FOR n = 2 TO 19
1020 PRINT AT n,30; PAPER 6; INK RND*5;CHR$ (137);CHR$
(134);AT n,0;CHR$ (137);CHR$ (134)
1030 NEXT n
1031 FOR n = 16 TO 170
1032 PLOT INK RND*6;INT (RND*200)+20,n
1036 NEXT n
1038 PRINT AT 0,7;"Astral Invaders  "; BRIGHT 1;AT 0,0; INK
2;"1 UP";AT 1,0; INK 7;"0";AT 0,25; INK 2;"Hi-Sc"; INK 7;AT
1,25;hisc
1039 FOR n=1 TO lives: PRINT AT 20,n; INK 6;CHR$ (144): NEXT
n: BEEP 1,4: BRIGHT 1
1040 LET i$=INKEY$
1060 IF i$="z" THEN LET x=x-1
1070 IF i$="x" THEN LET x=x+1
1080 PRINT AT 18,x;" ";CHR$ (144);" "
1090 IF i$=" " THEN GO SUB 3500: REM Firing
1100 GO SUB 3000: REM Bug movement
1110 IF ay = 19 THEN BEEP .1,2: LET ax=INT (RND*16)+6:
RANDOMIZE : LET lives=lives-1
1120 IF ay=19 THEN FOR n=1 TO lives: PRINT AT 20,n; INK 6;CHR$
(144);" ": NEXT n: LET ay=2
1130 IF lives=0 THEN GO SUB 2000
1300 GO TO 1040
2000 REM ***** DEAD
2010 PRINT AT 18,5; INK 2;"** BASE DESTROYED **"
2020 PRINT AT 10,10; FLASH 1;"PRESS TO RESTART"
2030 IF INKEY$="" THEN GO TO 2030
```

```
2050 GO TO 100
3000 REM *** move alien
3020 PRINT AT ay,ax;" "
3030 IF ay=9 OR ay=6 THEN LET ax=ax+INT ((RND*2)-(RND*2))
3050 LET ay=ay+1
3060 PRINT AT ay,ax; INK acol;CHR$ (alien): BEEP speed,ay-10
3070 IF score>200 THEN LET l$="L E V E L  T W O"
3080 IF speed > .01 THEN LET speed = speed - .01:
3400 RETURN
3500 REM ***** FIRING
3510 PLOT x*8+12,32: DRAW OVER 1; INK 2;0,100: DRAW OVER 1;0,-
100: PLOT INK 0;x*8+12,132
3520 BEEP .01,10
3530 IF x+1<>ax THEN RETURN
3540 FOR n =7 TO 0 STEP -1
3550 PRINT INK n;AT ay,ax;CHR$ (alien)
3560 BEEP .006,n*2
3570 NEXT n
3575 PRINT AT ay,ax;" "
3580 LET score = score + ((alien-144)*10):
3590 LET ax=INT (RND*16)+6: LET ay=2
3600 IF score> hisc THEN LET hisc=score
3610 PRINT AT 1,0;score;"   ";AT 1,25;hisc;"   "
3620 RANDOMIZE : LET acol=INT (RND*6)+1: LET alien = 145+INT
(RND*3)
3700 RETURN
5000 FOR n = 0 TO 31:
5010 READ dat
5020 POKE USR "a"+n,dat
5030 NEXT n
5050 RETURN
5100 DATA 24,24,189,219,189,165,129,0
5110 DATA 0,24,52,122,60,24,36,66
5120 DATA 60,126,219,219,255,255,153,66
5130 DATA 36,60,231,102,60,90,24,36
```

What's New?

We have setup and pre-drawn the screen and the gameplay movement overwrites some of the background but not much. This provides a nice colourful convincing game screen for our action shooter.

```
1110 IF ay = 19 THEN BEEP .1,2: LET ax=INT (RND*16)+6:
RANDOMIZE : LET lives=lives-1
```

Above we can see that if the Alien reaches the bottom of the screen we will forfeit a life.

```
3000 REM *** move alien
3020 PRINT AT ay,ax;" "
3030 IF ay=9 OR ay=6 THEN LET ax=ax+INT ((RND*2)-(RND*2))
3050 LET ay=ay+1
3060 PRINT AT ay,ax; INK acol;CHR$ (alien): BEEP speed,ay-10
3070 IF score>200 THEN LET l$="L E V E L   T W O"
3080 IF speed > .01 THEN LET speed = speed - .01:
3400 RETURN
```

Above section controls the Alien movement and adds some challenge by shifting the movement at certain points on the screen randomly.

```
3500 REM ***** FIRING
3510 PLOT x*8+12,32: DRAW OVER 1; INK 2;0,100: DRAW OVER 1;0,-
100: PLOT INK 0;x*8+12,132
3520 BEEP .01,10
3530 IF x+1<>ax THEN RETURN
3540 FOR n =7 TO 0 STEP -1
3550 PRINT INK n;AT ay,ax;CHR$ (alien)
3560 BEEP .006,n*2
3570 NEXT n
```

The above section will test our shooting. Again we use 8*value to do our PLOT and DRAW commands so we can position them with our UDGs (Sprites).

Remember: PLOT places your pen and DRAW makes the lines.

Suggestions for Extending (optional)

1] *Add more enemies to the game*
2] *Add more enemies attacking the player at the same time within a close proximity on the screen*
3] *Add more sound effects or change the graphics and theme of the whole game to one of your own*

COLOUR STACKS

This is a fun and addictive game, more fun that the name implies. I was playing around with prototyping different ideas when I came up with this simple but addictive puzzler. You have to avoid the wrong colours and watch your move counter but you have a limited amount of switches to change the colour. I am planning to release a mobile version of this game in the near future.

Players: 1

Rules: Puzzle game where the player must attach the block to the same colour without coming into contact with any other colours. The player has a move counter that increases if they complete correct matches.

Controls: q = up, a = down, o = left, p = right, [space] = switch colour.

```
 10 REM ******ZX Spectrum Code Club *******
 15 REM * COLOUR STACKS by Gary Plowman    *
 20 REM *************2015*****************
 30 INK 7: PAPER 0: BORDER 4: CLS
 45 REM ****** Initialising variables
 50 PRINT AT 2,10; INK 7; BRIGHT 1; PAPER 0;"COLOUR STACKS":
PRINT AT 4,5;"MATCH COL:OURS TOGETHER!";AT 6,5;"TOUCH A WRONG
COLOUR WILL";AT 8,5;"FORCE A RESTART!";AT 10,5;"[SPACE] to
change colour"
 80 PRINT AT 18,5; FLASH 1;"PRESS A KEY TO START": PAUSE 0
100 GO SUB 300: REM initialise
130 GO SUB 1000: REM main loop for game
200 GO TO 30:
300 REM ***** SETUP
```

```
 310 LET lives=3: LET score=0: LET misses=0: LET y=19: LET
x=24 : LET timer=50: LET setting=INT (RND*5)+1: LET r=0: LET
xx=0: LET yy=0: LET chg=3:
 320 RANDOMIZE
 390 RETURN
1000 CLS : REM ******* MAIN GAME:
1010 PLOT 10,10: INK 6: DRAW 0,150: DRAW 200,0: DRAW 0,-150:
DRAW -200,0
1020 GO SUB 2000: REM *** DRAW Board
1100 LET i$=INKEY$
1105 IF timer=0 THEN STOP
1106 PRINT AT 12,27;"Moves";AT 13,27;"Left";AT 15,27;timer;" "
1110 IF i$="" THEN GO TO 1100
1115 LET xx = x: LET yy= y: PRINT AT y,x; PAPER 0;" "
1120 IF i$="o" THEN LET x=x-1
1130 IF i$="p" THEN LET x=x+1
1140 IF i$="q" THEN LET y=y-1
1150 IF i$="a" THEN LET y=y+1
1055 IF x>24 OR x<2 THEN LET x=xx
1056 IF y>19 OR y<2 THEN LET y=yy
1160 IF i$=" " AND chg>0 THEN LET chg=chg-1: BEEP .3,3: LET
setting=INT (RND*5)+1
1170 GO SUB 3000 : REM test for colour
1180 LET timer=timer-1
1200 PRINT AT y,x; INK 7; PAPER setting;"O"
1900 GO TO 1100
2000 FOR n =1 TO 30
2010 PRINT AT INT (RND*13)+3,INT (RND*20)+2; PAPER INT
(RND*5)+1;" "
2030 NEXT n
2040 PRINT AT y,x; INK 7; PAPER setting;"O"
2050 RETURN
3000 REM **** fail if colour doesnt match
3010 LET att1=INT (ATTR (y,x+1)/8)
3020 LET att2=INT (ATTR (y,x-1)/8)
3030 LET att3=INT (ATTR (y-1,x)/8)
```

```
3040 LET att4=INT (ATTR (y+1,x)/8)
3060 IF att1 = setting OR att2=setting OR att3=setting OR
att4=setting THEN PRINT AT y,x; PAPER setting;" ": LET
score=score+setting: LET timer=timer+(setting*2): LET x=xx:
LET y=yy: LET setting=INT (RND*5)+1: BEEP .1,5: RETURN
3070 IF att1 > 0 OR att2>0 OR att3>0 OR att4>0 THEN PRINT
"Dead!": BEEP 1,-5: GO TO 10:ff
3080 PRINT AT 4,27;"SC";AT 6,27;score
3090 PRINT AT 0,2;"You have ";chg;" switches [SP] left"
3100 RETURN
```

What's New?

ATTR() function is similar to SCREEN$() but it returns the colour attributes for the screen location queried in the form of a numeric value. It's slightly more complex but much more useful where the collision detection cannot rely on SCREEN$(). SCREEN$() will not work with UDGs for instance. The workings of a the ATTR() function is harder to work out but here is the gist of it.

ATTR() is the sum of the following values of attributes for a single character position on the screen.

If the character position is flashing	=	128 otherwise 0
If the character position is bright	=	64 otherwise 0
Paper colour	=	colour value * 8 (e.g. Paper Cyan = 5*8 = 40)
Ink colour	=	colour value (e.g. Ink Red = 2)

So adding all of those attributes will tell you what value should be returned by ATTR() function. ATTR is lot more reliable than SCREEN$().

```
3010 LET att1=INT (ATTR (y,x+1)/8)
3020 LET att2=INT (ATTR (y,x-1)/8)
```

```
3030 LET att3=INT (ATTR (y-1,x)/8)
3040 LET att4=INT (ATTR (y+1,x)/8)
```

3010 to 3040 are checking all sides for collision with a colour other than black and if you do not match the colour it will be Game Over.

```
1180 LET timer=timer-1
```

Using a Timer in your game is a nice easy dynamic and puts the player on alert from the start. In this game we deduct the timer only when the player moves, so it is not a real time timer. Because our game is a puzzle game we allow the player to think about there next move. This could also be employed for a game where you needed to reduce a players energy when they move, requiring them to eat to get energy back.

Suggestions for Extending (optional)

1] Add more variation to the game – items to increase time
    could appear randomly
2] Add small maze sections to the game

ANGRY CHICKY

> *It's Christmas day and Young Timmy is hungry for his breakfast but needs some Eggs for his Eggy Bread and Eggnog. The chicken who laid the eggs is angry and looking to bite poor Timmy and prevent him taking the eggs! Guide Timmy to collect as many eggs as possible and advance to the next screen.*

Players: 1

Rules: Collect all the gold and avoid the traps and the Apache Indians.

Controls: q = up, a = down, o = left, p = right, also Joystick will work if you have one.

Bonus: As a little chore for you for the graphics try to work out on paper etc the BIN to Decimal values for the graphics to save you having to key in those 1s and 0s.

```
  10 REM ********ZX Spectrum Code Club ********
  15 REM * ANGRY CHICKY by G Plowman 2015        *
  20 REM *****************************************
  25 GO SUB 7000: REM **** Create graphics
  30 INK 1: PAPER 7: BORDER 4: CLS
  45 REM ****** Initialising variables
  50 PRINT AT 2,10; INK 7; BRIGHT 1; PAPER 2;"ANGRY CHICKY":
PRINT AT 4,5;"Help Timmy ";CHR$ (145);" grab eggs to
make his Eggy Bread";AT 6,5;"Avoid the Angry Chicky!!"; INK
2;CHR$ (146)
  35 LET lives=3
  60 PRINT AT 7,5;"Avoid the cracked ice!"; PAPER 5; INK 2;"x"
  65 PRINT AT 8,5;"Collect the EGGS!"; PAPER 6;"o"
```

69

```
  70 PRINT AT 11,2;"Controls: ";AT 12,2;"Q/A=Up/Down,
O/P=Left/Right"
  80 PRINT AT 18,5; FLASH 1;"PRESS A KEY TO START": PAUSE 0
 100 GO SUB 300: REM initialise
 130 GO SUB 1000: REM main loop for game
 200 GO TO 30:
 300 REM ***** SETUP
 310 LET x=10: LET y=10: LET vx=0: LET vy=0: LET score=0: LET
lvl=1: LET ax=1: LET ay=1: LET ax2=0: LET ay2=0: LET loot=0
 330 RETURN
1000 CLS
1010 FOR n = 0 TO 19:
1030 PRINT AT n,0;CHR$ (144);AT n,31;CHR$ (144)
1040 NEXT n
1045 FOR n=1 TO 30
1050 PRINT AT 0,n;CHR$ (144);AT 19,n;CHR$ (144)
1060 NEXT n:
1070 FOR n = 1 TO 20
1080 PRINT AT INT (RND*15)+3,INT (RND*25)+3; PAPER 5; INK
2;"x"
1085 NEXT n
1086 FOR n = 1 TO 5:
1087 PRINT AT INT (RND*15)+3,INT (RND*25)+3; PAPER 6;"o"
1090 NEXT n
1095 PRINT AT 20,1;"Eggy Bread: ";score
1100 LET i$=INKEY$: LET i=IN 31
1110 IF (i$="q" OR i=8) AND y>2 THEN LET vy=-1: LET vx=0
1120 IF (i$="a" OR i=4) AND y<19 THEN LET vy=1: LET vx=0
1130 IF (i$="o" OR i=2) AND x>2 THEN LET vx=-1: LET vy=0
1140 IF (i$="p" OR i=1) AND y<30 THEN LET vx=1: LET vy=0
1145 LET x=x+vx: LET y=y+vy
1150 IF x=0 THEN GO SUB 2000
1160 IF x=31 THEN GO SUB 2000
1170 IF y=19 THEN GO SUB 2000
1180 IF y=0 THEN GO SUB 2000
1185 LET a$=SCREEN$ (y,x)
```

```
1190 IF a$="x" OR (y=ay AND x=ax) THEN GO SUB 2000
1200 IF a$="o" THEN GO SUB 3000
1210 PRINT AT y,x;CHR$ (145)
1230 IF vx<>0 THEN PRINT AT y,x-vx;" "
1240 IF vy<>0 THEN PRINT AT y-vy,x;" "
1250 IF lvl>0 THEN GO SUB 3500
1300 GO TO 1100
1900 STOP
2000 PRINT AT 21,15;"DEAD!";AT 15,10; FLASH 1;"RESTARTING":
BEEP 2,1: PAUSE 1000
2100 GO TO 30
3000 REM *** * Collect loot
3010 LET score = score +(INT (RND*4)+1)
3020 PRINT AT 20,1; PAPER 6; INK 2;"Eggy Bread: ";score: BEEP
.05,20
3030 LET loot=loot+1
3040 IF loot=5 THEN PRINT AT 15,10; FLASH 1;"NEXT ROUND!":
BEEP 2,1
3050 IF loot=5 THEN LET loot=0: LET lvl=lvl+1: LET ax=2: LET
ay=2: LET vx=0: LET vy=0: GO TO 1000
3060 RETURN
3500 REM **** Move Chicky
3505 LET ax2=ax: LET ay2=ay
3510 IF ax>x THEN PRINT AT ay,ax;" ": LET ax=ax-1: GO TO 3550:
3530 IF ax<x THEN PRINT AT ay,ax;" ": LET ax=ax+1: GO TO 3550
3520 IF ay<y THEN PRINT AT ay,ax;" ": LET ay=ay+1.2: GO TO
3550
3540 IF ay>y THEN PRINT AT ay,ax;" ": LET ay=ay-1.2
3550 IF SCREEN$ (ay,ax)<>" " THEN LET ax=ax2: LET ay=ay2:
3560 PRINT AT ay,ax; INK 2;CHR$ (146):
3565 IF ax=x AND ABS (ay-y)<1.5 THEN GO TO 2000
3590 RETURN
7000 FOR n = 0 TO 23
7010 READ dat
7020 POKE USR "a"+n,dat
7030 NEXT n
```

```
7040 RETURN
7050 DATA BIN 00111100
7060 DATA BIN 01000011
7070 DATA BIN 10110101
7080 DATA BIN 11000011
7090 DATA BIN 10000001
7110 DATA BIN 10000001
7120 DATA BIN 01000010
7130 DATA BIN 00111100
7150 DATA BIN 00111100
7160 DATA BIN 01111000
7165 DATA BIN 01100111
7170 DATA BIN 00100100
7180 DATA BIN 10111101
7210 DATA BIN 11111111
7220 DATA BIN 11000011
7230 DATA BIN 00000000
7350 DATA BIN 00111000
7360 DATA BIN 00110110
7365 DATA BIN 01111111
7370 DATA BIN 11100101
7380 DATA BIN 11011000
7410 DATA BIN 10111110
7420 DATA BIN 01111111
7430 DATA BIN 00111100
```

Fun Themes

A fun game with a funny premise. That is what a lot of the old spectrum classics have in common. Games like Mathew Smith's Manic Miner and Jet Set Willy, British gaming is literally full of games that were based on wacky ideas. Don't be afraid to experiment and have fun when making your games.

What's New?

We have used the ABS() function in our code, this is useful for calculating distances of objects from one another, amongst other things. This function returns the result as an absolute value, i.e. converting it to positive. So -1 become 1 and +1 is 1. This allows you test for difference between two values without the need of worrying if the value tested is +2 or -2. The use case in our Angry Chicky game is to find out if Chicky has caught Timmy.

Suggestions for Extending (optional)

1]   *Add another Angry Chicky to chase you*
2]   *Add more items to collect*
3]   *Add a timer bonus score to encourage the user to complete the screen quicker*

ALLOTMENT WARS

In this odd game you have to make money from your produce and compete with your opposing allotments by sabotaging each others veg. Throw weeds at the opponents allotment to reduce the supply of veg! Harking back to the mad days of bedroom coding zaniness that made British gaming great! This game is not in that league, but don't disregard weird ideas right away, some very successful indie games sound terrible on paper. This game is made for extending or changing so feel free to take apart and add extra features etc.

Players: 1

Rules: Throw weeds to hit other opponents Veg. Each shot you take lets one of the opponents get a shot back at you. You lose if you score goes below -4 and win the round   if your score is 5 or more.

Controls: Keys A – G or 1 to 7 will place your Gardener. Then A = Across, U = Up, D = Diagonal

```
  10 REM ********************************
  20 REM * ALLOTMENT WARS - Gary Plowman   *
  25 REM ********************************
  30 INK 7: PAPER 0: BORDER 0
  45 GO SUB 5000
  50 CLS : PRINT AT 2,10; INK 6; BRIGHT 1; PAPER 1;"ALLOTMENT
WARS": LET lvl = 10: LET round=1
  60 PRINT AT 4,1;"You must win Best Allotment"
  70 PRINT AT 6,1;"Throw weeds to spoil opp. Veg  "
  75 PRINT AT 8,1;"Score 5 to get to next round!";AT
10,1;"Each Veg you hit will give you an extra Veg"
```

```
  80 PRINT AT 18,5; FLASH 1;"PRESS A KEY TO START": PAUSE 0:
CLS : RANDOMIZE
 110 GO SUB 300: REM initialise
 130 GO SUB 1000: REM draw screen
 140 GO SUB 3000: REM draw info on screen
 150 GO SUB 2000: main loop
 160 GO TO 50
 300 REM **** Setup
 310 LET score1=0: DIM v(3): LET score2=0: LET score3=0: LET
score4=0
 320 LET power=0: LET rightpos=0: LET toppos=0: LET g$="CPBT":
LET targ=0: LET turn=1
 400 RETURN
1000 REM **** Screen
1005 PRINT AT 1,23;"ALLOTMENT";AT 2,25;"WARS"
1010 FOR n=1 TO 7
1020 PRINT AT n,5; PAPER 4;"-*-*-*-";
1030 PRINT AT n+10,5; PAPER 4;"-*-*-*-"; PAPER 0;n
1040 PRINT AT n,15; PAPER 4;"-*-*-*-";
1050 PRINT AT n+10,15; PAPER 4;"-*-*-*-";
1080 NEXT n
1085 RANDOMIZE
1090 PRINT AT 7,12; INK 3;CHR$ (144);AT 7,14; INK 5;CHR$
(144);AT 10,20; INK 2;CHR$ (144)
1100 PRINT AT 10,5;"ABCDEFG";AT 19,0;"GROWING VEG - PLEASE
WAIT..."
1120 PRINT AT 9,13; INK 6;CHR$ (144)
1140 REM ******* WE ADD SOME VEG
1150 FOR n = 1 TO 18
1160 FOR m = 1 TO 20
1165 LET rn =INT (RND*lvl)+1
1170 IF SCREEN$ (n,m)="*" AND rn<5 THEN PRINT AT n,m; PAPER 4;
INK 3;g$(rn)
1180 NEXT m
1190 NEXT n
1500 RETURN
```

```
2000 REM **** Main Loop
2010 LET a$=INKEY$
2020 IF a$="" THEN GO TO 2010
2030 IF a$>="1" AND a$<="7" THEN LET rightpos = VAL a$: GO SUB
2500: GO SUB 3000
2040 IF a$>="a" AND a$<="g" THEN LET toppos = CODE a$-96: GO
SUB 2500: GO SUB 3000
2100 GO TO 2010
2500 REM **** Throw weeds
2505 PRINT AT 10,13;" ": BEEP .05,4
2510 IF rightpos>0 THEN PRINT AT 10+rightpos,13; INK 6;CHR$
(144): PRINT AT 10,13;" "
2515 IF toppos>0 THEN PRINT AT 9,4+toppos; INK 6;CHR$ (144):
PRINT AT 10,13;" "
2520 PRINT AT 19,0;"Fire (A)cross (U)p or (D)iagonal";AT
9,13;" "
2540 LET power=power+1: PRINT AT  20,0;"Pwr:"
2550 LET b$=INKEY$
2560 PRINT INK 2;AT 20,3+power;" ";CHR$ (138)
2570 IF power > 8 THEN LET power = 1
2580 IF b$="a" OR b$="u" OR b$="d" THEN GO TO 2600
2590 GO TO 2540:
2600 BEEP .05,4: LET fx=0: LET fy=0
2610 FOR n = power TO 1 STEP -.5
2620 BEEP .05,n
2630 NEXT n
2650 IF rightpos>0 AND b$="a" THEN LET fx= 13+power: LET
fy=10+rightpos
2660 IF rightpos>0 AND b$="u" THEN LET fx=13: LET
fy=10+rightpos-power
2670 IF rightpos>0 AND b$="d" THEN LET fx=13+power: LET
fy=10+rightpos-power
2680 IF toppos>0 AND b$="a" THEN LET fx=4+toppos+power: LET
fy=9
2690 IF toppos>0 AND b$="u" THEN LET fx=4+toppos: LET fy=9-
power
```

```
2700 IF toppos>0 AND b$="d" THEN LET fx=4+toppos+power: LET
fy=9-power
2710 LET r$=SCREEN$ (fy,fx)
2710 PRINT AT fy,fx; INK 6;"."
2715 IF fx<12 THEN LET targ=1
2720 IF fx>12 AND fy<9 THEN LET targ=2
2730 IF fx>12 AND fy>9 THEN LET targ=3:
2735 LET rightpos=0: LET toppos=0
2740 IF r$="C" OR r$="P" OR r$="B" OR r$="T" THEN LET
score1=score1+1: BEEP .5,9: LET vgx=5: LET vgy=11: GO SUB 3200
2745 GO SUB 3300
2750 RETURN
3000 REM **** Redraw INFO *******
3010 PRINT AT 9,5;"              "
3020 FOR n = 1 TO 9
3030 PRINT AT 8+n,13;" "
3040 NEXT n
3050 PRINT AT 19,0;"Select A - G or 1 - 7            ";AT
20,0;"                         "
3060 PRINT AT 3,23; INK 6;"You: ";CHR$ (96);score1;" ";AT
4,23; INK 3;"Purp:";CHR$ (96);v(1);" ";AT 5,23; INK
5;"Blue:";CHR$ (96);v(2);" ";AT 6,23; INK 2;"Red: ";CHR$
(96);v(3);" ";
3070 PRINT AT 9,13; INK 6;CHR$ (144)
3075 PRINT AT 8,23;"ROUND:";round
3080 IF score1<-2 OR score1>4 THEN GO SUB 3400:
3090 RETURN
3200 REM **** WIN SOME VEG
3201 LET cnt=0
3205 IF targ> 0 THEN LET v(targ)=v(targ)-1
3206 IF targ=0 THEN LET v(turn)=v(turn)+1
3210 LET vegx=vgx+INT (RND*8): LET vegy=vgy+INT (RND*8): REM
LET vg =INT (RND*4)+1
3220 IF SCREEN$ (vegy,vegx)="*" THEN PRINT AT vegy,vegx; PAPER
4; INK 1;r$: RETURN
3225 LET cnt = cnt + 1
```

```
3226 IF cnt > 40 THEN RETURN
3230 GO TO 3210
3240 RETURN
3300 REM *** Enemy shoot
3304 BEEP .4,3: PRINT AT 19,0;"Opponents throws weed!
"
3310 FOR n = 10 TO 1 STEP -1: BEEP .06,n: NEXT n:
3315 LET fx = 5+INT (RND*7): LET fy=11+INT (RND*7):
3320 IF turn=1 THEN LET vgx =5 : LET vgy =1
3330 IF turn=2 THEN LET vgx =15 : LET vgy =1
3340 IF turn=3 THEN LET vgx =15 : LET vgy =11
3350 LET r$=SCREEN$ (fy,fx)
3360 PRINT AT fy,fx; INK 6;"."
3370 IF r$="C" OR r$="P" OR r$="B" OR r$="T" THEN LET
score1=score1-1: LET targ=0: BEEP .5,9: GO SUB 3200
3380 LET turn=turn+1
3385 IF turn>3 THEN LET turn=1
3390 RETURN
3400 REM WIN OR LOSE
3410 IF score1 < -2 THEN PRINT AT 10,10; FLASH 1;"UH! OH! YOU
LOSE!": BEEP 1,0: PAUSE 0: GO TO 50
3420 IF score1> 4 THEN PRINT AT 10,10; FLASH 1;"NEXT ROUND!":
LET round = round + 1: LET lvl = lvl +3: BEEP 1,10: PAUSE 0:
CLS : GO TO 110
3430 IF lvl>25 THEN LET lvl = 25:
5000 FOR n = 0 TO 7
5010 READ dat
5020 POKE USR "a"+n,dat
5030 NEXT n
5040 RETURN
5050 DATA 24,126,24,24,10,60,56,8
```

What's New?

The original concept for this game changed a few times. In the end I went away from an action based game to a turn-based one. This was purely due to the Spectrum's limits and playability. This one offers more options to extend over the arcade version. If you wish you can convert / re-write to a multiplayer (hotseat) game for 1 to four players, while keeping remaining players as CPU controlled.

Reducing code

We were able to reduce the number of IF statements for keypresses by using code that translated the keypress information into coordinates for our game.

```
2030 IF a$>="1" AND a$<="7" THEN LET rightpos = VAL a$: GO SUB
2500: GO SUB 3000
2040 IF a$>="a" AND a$<="g" THEN LET toppos = CODE a$-96: GO
SUB 2500: GO SUB 3000
```

VAL converts string numbers to actual numbers and CODE returns the character set value for a string character.

Suggestions for Extending (optional)

1]   Add more features – e.g. multiplayer
2]   Make the veg type matter – give different score per veg
3]   Maybe you could add random events that affect the game

RETRO HUNTER

Little Ally has gone to a Retro Gaming Expo and must try to collect as many games as he can within his time limit. He is slightly bonkers and runs in one direction until he reaches a stall or the wall of the building. The more games he can collect, the more time will be added to his timer. However, other Retro Collectors are here and looking to snap up retro games too. So he's gotta be quick to figure out how to get around the Play Expo in this fun little Puzzle game.

Players: 2

Rules: Navigate the location and use the other stalls to help you reach the areas to collect your games.

Controls: q = up, a = down, o = left, p = right to move.

```
 10 REM ******ZX Spectrum Code Club *******
 15 REM * RETRO HUNTER by Gary Plowman     *
 20 REM *************2015*****************
 30 INK 0: PAPER 5: BORDER 1: CLS
 40 GO SUB 6000
 50 PRINT AT 2,10; INK 7; BRIGHT 1; PAPER 0;"RETRO HUNTER"
 60 PRINT AT 4,5;"Collect games to succeed!";AT
5,5;"Collections increase Timer!"
 80 PRINT AT 18,5; FLASH 1;"PRESS A KEY TO START": PAUSE 0:
CLS : RANDOMIZE
110 GO SUB 300: REM initialise:
130 GO SUB 1000: REM draw screen
140 GO SUB 2000: REM main loop
300 REM *******
```

```
 310 LET x= 7: LET y=17: LET vy=0: LET vx=0: LET sega=0: LET
nin=0: LET spec=0: LET comm=0: LET timer=100
 400 RETURN
1000 REM ****** Screen
1010 CLS : INK 5: PAPER 5: PRINT INK 0;AT 0,4;"RUN AROUND PLAY
EXPO HALL";AT 1,4;"COLLECTING RETRO GAMES!" ;AT 20,0;"*RETRO
HUNTER*"
1020 PRINT AT 03,5;"MMMMMMMMMMMMM"
1030 PRINT AT 04,5;"MM          MM"
1040 PRINT AT 05,5;"M  M  M      M"
1050 PRINT AT 06,5;"M   M  MMM   M"
1060 PRINT AT 07,5;"MM      M    M"
1070 PRINT AT 08,5;"M   M       MM"
1080 PRINT AT 09,5;"M  MMMM M    M"
1090 PRINT AT 10,5;"M      M     M"
1100 PRINT AT 11,5;"MMM          M"
1110 PRINT AT 12,5;"M            M"
1120 PRINT AT 13,5;"M         MMM"
1130 PRINT AT 14,5;"MM   M  M    M"
1140 PRINT AT 15,5;"M    MM      M"
1145 PRINT AT 16,5;"M   MMM      M"
1140 PRINT AT 17,5;"M         M  M"
1150 PRINT AT 18,5;"MMMMMMMMMMMMM"
1160 FOR n=3 TO 18
1170 FOR m = 5 TO 18
1180 IF SCREEN$ (n,m)="M" THEN PRINT AT n,m; PAPER 1; INK
1;;"M"
1190 NEXT m: NEXT n
1200 INK 2: PRINT AT 3,20;"SEGA: ";sega;AT 5,20;"Nndo:
";nin;AT 7,20;"ZXSp: ";spec;AT 9,20;"C-64: ";comm
1210 LET score= nin+spec+sega+comm
1220 IF score<10 THEN LET s$="Novice"
1230 IF score>=10 THEN LET s$="Beginner"
1240 IF score>30 THEN LET s$="RetroFan"
1250 IF score>50 THEN LET s$="RetroGuru!"
1280 PRINT AT 18,20;s$;" "
```

```
1300 RETURN
2000 REM GAME LOOP
2010 LET i$=INKEY$: LET j=IN 31
2110 IF (i$="q" OR j=8) AND (vx=0 AND vy=0) THEN LET vy=-1:
LET vx=0
2120 IF (i$="a" OR j=4) AND (vx=0 AND vy=0) THEN LET vy=1: LET
vx=0
2140 IF (i$="o" OR j=1) AND (vx=0 AND vy=0) THEN LET vx=-1:
LET vy=0
2130 IF (i$="p" OR j=2) AND (vx=0 AND vy=0) THEN LET vx=1: LET
vy=0
2190 IF SCREEN$ (y+vy,x+vx)<>"M" THEN PRINT AT y,x;" ": LET
x=x+vx: LET y=y+vy
2192 IF SCREEN$ (y+vy,x+vx)="M" THEN LET vx=0: LET vy=0
2195 LET y$=SCREEN$ (y,x)
2200 IF y$="S" THEN LET sega = sega +1: LET timer=timer+20:
BEEP .2,8: GO SUB 1200
2210 IF y$="C" THEN LET comm = comm+1: LET timer=timer+10:
BEEP .2,5: GO SUB 1200
2220 IF y$="Z" THEN LET spec = spec +1: LET timer=timer+30:
BEEP .2,13: GO SUB 1200
2230 IF y$="N" THEN LET nin = nin +1: LET timer=timer+20: BEEP
.2,8: GO SUB 1200
2240 IF timer> 160 THEN LET timer=160:
2290 PRINT AT y,x; INK 0;CHR$ (144);AT 20,20;"Clock:";timer;"
"
2300 LET timer=timer-1
2310 IF timer <= 0 THEN PRINT AT 10,10;"GAME OVER";AT
12,10;"SCORE WAS ";score: BEEP 2,10: CLS : GO TO 50
2400 IF INT (RND*100)<6 THEN GO SUB 3100
2410 IF INT (RND*50)<20 THEN GO SUB 3200
3000 GO TO 2000
3100 REM ***** PLACE COLLECTABLE
3110 LET cx=6+INT (RND*10): LET cy=4+INT (RND*10): LET ty=INT
(RND*4)+1
3120 IF SCREEN$ (cy,cx)="M" THEN GO TO 3110
```

```
3130 IF ty=1 THEN LET t$="S"
3140 IF ty=2 THEN LET t$="N"
3150 IF ty=3 THEN LET t$="C"
3160 IF ty=4 THEN LET t$="Z":
3170 PRINT AT cy,cx; INK ty-1;t$:
3190 RETURN
3200 REM ***** MOVE OTHER COLLECTORS
3210 LET cx=6+INT (RND*10): LET cy=4+INT (RND*10)
3220 LET c$=SCREEN$ (cy,cx)
3230 IF c$="S" OR c$="Z" OR c$="N" OR c$="C" THEN PRINT AT
cy,cx; INK 2;CHR$ (144): BEEP .3,-3:
3250 RETURN
6000 FOR n = 0 TO 7
6010 READ dat
6020 POKE USR "a"+n,dat
6030 NEXT n
6040 RETURN
6100 DATA  8,20,95,62,62,28,20,20
```

Puzzle Games

These type of games work very well in Sinclair BASIC. They usually don't rely on fast paced action and require more thinking and analysis. You can change this game in many ways and have it resemble a another theme that is of interest to you or of interest to someone in your family. Changing the screen level is simply done by altering lines 1020 to 1150. Also only a few changes are required to make a simple maze game from this base code.

```
1020 PRINT AT 03,5;"MMMMMMMMMMMMM"
1030 PRINT AT 04,5;"MM         MM"
1040 PRINT AT 05,5;"M  M  M     M"
1050 PRINT AT 06,5;"M   M  MMM  M"
1060 PRINT AT 07,5;"MM      M   M"
```

```
1070 PRINT AT 08,5;"M    M        MM"
1080 PRINT AT 09,5;"M  MMMM M    M"
1090 PRINT AT 10,5;"M      M      M"
1100 PRINT AT 11,5;"MMM          M"
1110 PRINT AT 12,5;"M            M"
1120 PRINT AT 13,5;"M          MMM"
1130 PRINT AT 14,5;"MM   M  M    M"
1140 PRINT AT 15,5;"M    MM       M"
1145 PRINT AT 16,5;"M  MMM       M"
1140 PRINT AT 17,5;"M          M  M"
1150 PRINT AT 18,5;"MMMMMMMMMMMMM"
```

Making your game fun

Everyone wants to make a fun game. But the concept can sound a lot more fun than the end result. The game Retro Hunter started out with your character Ally collecting on the screen against the clock but it had no real challenge as just a running maze game. The end version became a puzzle game with only small tweaks to the code and a redesign of the screen map. So re-thinking your ideas is be better than scrapping a game completely. And this is a lot more fun now.

Suggestions for Extending (optional)

1]   *Make your own map and theme using the same mechanics*
2]   *Increase the screen size*
3]   *Add a 2 player mode with each taking turns to move to collect games*

SNOWBALL SHOOTOUT

No list of games is complete without a Christmas themed game to enjoy in the festive season. Try to beat the other team by scoring 5 snowballs first. Choose the shooter then choose two members of your team to hide.

Players: 2

Rules: Choose a Shooter and then two of your team to hide. Be careful to hide your key presses from your opponent.

Controls: Keys 1 to 4.

```
 10 REM ******** ZX Spectrum Code Club *********
 15 REM * SNOWBALL SHOOTOUT by G Plowman 2015  *
 18 REM *****************************************
 20 BRIGHT 1: INK 2: PAPER 7: BORDER 4 : CLS
 30 GO SUB 5000: REM *** graphics
 40 GO SUB 200: REM *** Setup
 50 GO SUB 300: REM *** Restart
 60 GO SUB 1000: REM *** Main loop:
200 LET score=0: DIM p(4): DIM o(4): LET turn=1: LET
shoot1=0: LET shoot2=0: LET sc1=0: LET sc2=0: LET hide=0
210 FOR n = 1 TO 4
220 LET p(n)=0: LET o(n)=0
250 RETURN
300 PRINT AT 6,5;"Snowball Shootout!"
310 PRINT AT 8,5;"Winter Is Coming!";AT 10,5;"EACH TURN:";AT
12,5;"Choose your player to shoot";AT 16,3; FLASH 1;"PRESS A
KEY TO START":
320 BEEP 1,4: PAUSE 0: CLS
```

```
 390 RETURN
1000 REM *** Main loop / Setup screen
1005 LET hide=0
1010 FOR n =1 TO 20 STEP 2
1020 PRINT INK 4;AT n,0;CHR$ (146);AT n,30;CHR$ (146)
1030 PRINT INK 4;AT n+1,0;CHR$ (147);AT n+1,30;CHR$ (147)
1040 NEXT n:
1050 FOR n = 0 TO 30
1060 PRINT INK 4;AT 0,n;CHR$ (147);AT 20,n;CHR$ (146)
1070 NEXT n:
1110 PRINT AT 3,7;"                    ";AT 4,7;"
"
1112 PRINT AT 17,7;"                    ";AT 18,7;"
"
1115 FOR n =1 TO 4
1120 PRINT INK 4;AT 4,6+n*3;CHR$ (146);AT 16,6+n*3;CHR$
(146);" "
1130 PRINT INK 4;AT 5,6+n*3;CHR$ (147);AT 17,6+n*3;CHR$
(147);" ":
1140 NEXT n
1150 FOR n = 1 TO 4
1155 IF p(n)=10 THEN GO TO 1165
1160 PRINT INK n+1;AT 3,7+n*3;CHR$ (145)
1165 IF o(n)=10 THEN GO TO 1185
1170 PRINT INK n;AT 18,7+n*3;CHR$ (145)
1185 NEXT n:
1190 PRINT AT 10,5; INK 1; PAPER 4;"BEGIN SNOWFIGHT!": PAUSE
0: GO SUB 3000: REM clear part of screen
1200 REM *** game loop
1205 LET hide=0
1210 IF turn=1 THEN PRINT AT 10,5; INK 1; PAPER 4;"PLAYER 1:
";AT 11,5;"PRESS 1-4 FOR :shooter ";AT 3,2; PAPER 7;"PLY 2";AT
18,2; PAPER 4;"PLY 1"
1210 IF turn=2 THEN PRINT AT 10,5; INK 1; PAPER 4;"PLAYER 2:
";AT 11,5;"PRESS 1-4 FOR :shooter ";AT 18,2; PAPER 7;"PLY
1";AT 3,2; PAPER 4;"PLY 2";
```

```
1215 PRINT AT 3,26;"SC:";AT 4,26;sc2;;AT 18,26;"SC:";AT
19,26;sc1
1220 LET i$=INKEY$: LET v=0
1225 IF i$>="1" AND i$<="4" THEN LET v=VAL i$: GO TO 1240
1230 GO TO 1220
1240 IF v<1 AND v>4 THEN BEEP .4,0: REM ** wrong!
1250 IF p(v)<11 AND turn=1 THEN BEEP .1,12: LET p(v)=1: GO TO
1280
1260 IF o(v)<11 AND turn=2 THEN BEEP .1,12: LET o(v)=1: GO TO
1280
1270 GO TO 1220
1280 LET i$=INKEY$: LET v=0: REM ** Select who is to take
cover
1285 IF i$>="1" AND i$<="4" THEN LET v=VAL i$
1290 IF turn=1 THEN PRINT AT 10,5; INK 1; PAPER 4;"PLAYER 1:
";AT 11,5;"PRESS 1-4 to Take Cover"
1292 IF turn=2 THEN PRINT AT 10,5; INK 1; PAPER 4;"PLAYER 2:
";AT 11,5;"PRESS 1-4 to Take Cover"
1295 IF v=0 THEN GO TO 1280
1300 IF v>=1 AND v<=4 AND turn=1 AND p(v)<10 THEN GO TO 1360
1310 IF v>=1 AND v<=4 AND turn=2 AND o(v)<10 THEN GO TO 1350
1330 GO TO 1280:
1350 IF o(v)=0 AND turn=2 THEN BEEP .1,8: LET o(v)=2: LET
hide=hide+1
1360 IF p(v)=0 AND turn=1 THEN BEEP .1,8: LET p(v)=2: LET
hide=hide+1
1370 GO SUB 3400
1390 IF turn=1 AND (check1=5) AND hide=2 THEN LET turn=2: GO
TO 1200
1400 IF turn=2 AND (check2=5) AND hide=2 THEN BEEP .4,4: GO
SUB 3000: GO SUB 2000:
1450 GO TO 1280
1600 REM *** Redraw Teams:
1610 FOR n=1 TO 4
1620 IF p(n)=1 THEN PRINT AT 18,7+n*3;" ";AT 17,7+n*3; INK
n;CHR$ (145)
```

```
1630 IF o(n)=1 THEN PRINT AT 3,7+n*3;" ";AT 4,7+n*3; INK
n+1;CHR$ (145)
1640 IF p(n)=0 THEN PRINT AT 18,7+n*3;" ";AT 17,7+n*3;" ";AT
18,7+n*3; INK n;CHR$ (145)
1650 IF o(n)=0 THEN PRINT AT 3,7+n*3;" ";AT 4,7+n*3;" ";AT
3,7+n*3; INK n;CHR$ (145)
1660 IF p(n)=2 THEN PRINT AT 18,7+n*3;" ";AT 18,6+n*3; INK
n+1;CHR$ (145)
1670 IF o(n)=2 THEN PRINT AT 3,7+n*3;" ";AT 3,6+n*3; INK
n;CHR$ (145)
1690 NEXT n
1700 RETURN
2000 REM *** NEXT Turn
2010 GO SUB 1600
2020 FOR n = 1 TO 4
2030 IF p(n)=1 THEN LET shoot1=n
2040 IF o(n)=1 THEN LET shoot2=n
2050 NEXT n
2060 REM *** shoot
2070 FOR n = 1 TO 13
2080 PRINT AT 16-n+1,7+shoot1*3;" ":
2090 PRINT AT 5+n-1,7+shoot2*3;" "
2100 PRINT AT 16-n,7+shoot1*3;CHR$ (144)
2110 PRINT AT 5+n,7+shoot2*3;CHR$ (144)
2120 BEEP .1,n
2140 NEXT n
2150 IF o(shoot1)<2 THEN BEEP 1,12: PRINT AT
3,7+shoot1*3;"ow!": LET o(shoot1)=10: LET sc1=sc1+1
2150 IF p(shoot2)<2 THEN BEEP 1,12: PRINT AT
18,7+shoot2*3;"ow!": LET p(shoot2)=10: LET sc2=sc2+1
2200 LET turn = 1
2210 REM PRINT AT 11,3;"NEXT ROUND!!":
2220 FOR n=1 TO 4
2230 IF o(n)<11 THEN LET o(n)=0
2240 IF p(n)<11 THEN LET p(n)=0
2250 NEXT n
```

```
2260 GO SUB 3400: REM ** check team
2270 IF sc2>=5 AND sc1<sc2 THEN PRINT AT 10,10;"PLAYER 1
LOST!": PAUSE 100: BEEP 1,10: PAUSE 0: CLS : GO TO 40
2280 IF sc1>=5 AND sc2<sc1 THEN PRINT AT 10,10;"PLAYER 2
LOST!": PAUSE 100: BEEP 1,10: PAUSE 0: CLS : GO TO 40
2290 GO TO 1110
2300 RETURN
3000 REM *** Clear screen routine
3010 PRINT AT 10,3;"                        "
3020 PRINT AT 11,3;"                        "
3030 RETURN
3400 REM *** Checking teams routine
3410 LET check1=p(1)+p(2)+p(3)+p(4)
3420 LET check2=o(1)+o(2)+o(3)+o(4)
3450 RETURN
5000 FOR n = 0 TO 31:
5010 READ dat
5020 POKE USR "a"+n,dat
5030 NEXT n
5050 RETURN
5100 DATA 0,24,52,122,60,24,0,0
5110 DATA 24,60,102,102,60,219,24,36
5120 DATA 8,28,28,42,73,28,42,73
5130 DATA 28,42,73,28,42,73,28,62
```

Progress

If you've gotten this far you must be really getting to grips with BASIC and learning intuitively what most of the BASIC commands do. Also you must be familiar now with coding in a simple template for a new game.

That's how I learned to code!

What's New?

Loops are very handy for doing a lot of work with very little code. An easy way to think of it is "count from 1 to 13" is the FOR n=x to y and the NEXT n part seals the loop by jumping back to increase the count. Other languages have other types of loops but the FOR NEXT loop was the original one in Sinclair BASIC.

```
2070 FOR n = 1 TO 13
2080 PRINT AT 16-n+1,7+shoot1*3;" ":
2090 PRINT AT 5+n-1,7+shoot2*3;" "
2100 PRINT AT 16-n,7+shoot1*3;CHR$ (144)
2110 PRINT AT 5+n,7+shoot2*3;CHR$ (144)
2120 BEEP .1,n
2140 NEXT n
```

The above code creates the shooting effect in the game. You can count backwards also providing you use something like…

```
2070 FOR n = 13 TO 1 STEP -1
```

It's not always the best choice if the loop is small. Looping from 1 to 2 is not usually done. Also keep in mind the commands you have within your loop, slow commands can really slow down your code if they happen to be included in a loop for no good reason or by mistake.

Suggestions for Extending (optional)

1]   Add more sound effects or change the graphics and theme
of the whole game to one of your own e.g. Cowboys

TETRIX

Inspired by another super game that was extremely popular and is still played today. The amazing Russian game Tetris that broke records across the world and shipped with the hugely successful Game Boy hand held from Nintendo. Still the best hand held game system that ever was! In my humble opinion. Our version will have a little bit more colour to it. I hope you enjoy this simplified version of the gaming classic that came from behind the Iron Curtain. Nostrovia!

Players: 1

Rules: Make complete lines to get points and free up the screen.

Controls: z = left, x = right, space will rotate some of the block shapes.

```
  10 REM ******ZX Spectrum Code Club *******
  15 REM * TETRIX by Gary Plowman    2015   *
  20 REM *********************************
  30 INK 0: PAPER 7: BORDER 4
  45 REM ****** Initialising variables
  50 PRINT AT 2,10; INK 7; BRIGHT 1; PAPER 0;"TETRIX": PRINT
AT 4,5;""
  60 PRINT AT 4,5;"Mistakes cost Points!"
  80 PRINT AT 18,5; FLASH 1;"PRESS A KEY TO START": PAUSE 0:
CLS
 100 GO SUB 5000: REM Graphics
 110 GO SUB 300: REM initialise:
 130 GO SUB 1000: REM draw screen
 140 GO SUB 2000: main loop:
 300 LET blocktype=0: LET rotate=0: LET inkcol=0: LET ypos=4:
LET xpos=INT (RND*10)+7: LET rotateproc=3000
```

```
 310 DIM a(3): DIM b(3): DIM c$(3): DIM  d$(3):
 330 LET xpos2=0: LET score=0: LET offset=0: LET mov=0: LET
lines=0
 340 GO SUB 3000
 360 RETURN
1000 REM ****** Screen
1010 FOR n = 6 TO 16: PRINT AT 19,n; PAPER 4; INK 6;CHR$
(146): NEXT n
1020 FOR m =2 TO 19
1030 PRINT AT m,5; PAPER 4; INK 6;CHR$ (146);CHR$ (146);AT
m,16;CHR$ (146);CHR$ (146)
1030 NEXT m
1040 PRINT AT 4,20; PAPER 1; INK 6;"LINES";AT 5,20;lines
1100 RETURN
2000 REM *** MAIN GAME
2005 GO SUB 3600
2008 IF mov=1 THEN GO SUB 3700
2010 LET i$=INKEY$:
2016 LET mov=0
2020 LET atr1=ATTR (ypos,xpos): LET atr2=ATTR (ypos+1,xpos):
LET atr11=ATTR (ypos,xpos+1): LET atr12=ATTR (ypos+1,xpos+1):
LET atr21=ATTR (ypos,xpos+2): LET atr22=ATTR (ypos+1,xpos+2):
2030 IF blocktype<=2 AND (atr1=56 OR atr2=56) AND (atr11=56 OR
atr12=56) AND (atr21=56 OR atr22=56) THEN LET mov=1
2040 IF blocktype>2 AND (atr1=56 OR atr2=56) AND (atr11=56 OR
atr12=56) THEN LET mov=1
2050 IF mov=1 AND i$="z" AND xpos>7 AND ATTR (ypos,xpos-1)=56
THEN GO SUB 3600: LET xpos=xpos-1: LET offset=1
2060 IF mov=1 AND i$="x" AND ((atr11=56 AND ATTR (ypos-
1,xpos+1)=56) OR (atr21=56 AND ATTR (ypos-1,xpos+2)=56) OR
(ATTR (ypos,xpos+3)=56 AND ATTR (ypos-1,xpos+3)=56)) THEN GO
SUB 3600: LET xpos=xpos+1: LET offset=-1
2070 IF i$=" " AND mov=1 THEN GO SUB 4800
2100 LET ypos=ypos+mov
2110 IF mov=0 THEN GO SUB 3500: GO SUB 3000
2205 GO TO 2000
```

```
2210 GO SUB 3000
2600 GO TO 2000
3000 REM rotateoproc
3005 GO SUB 4000: GO SUB 4000: RANDOMIZE
3006 FOR n = 1 TO 3: LET b(n)=0: LET a(n)=0: LET c$(n)="": LET
d$(n)="": NEXT n
3007 IF ypos < 4 THEN BEEP .5,-4: PRINT AT 10,10;"GAME OVER":
PAUSE 0: PAUSE 0: CLS : GO TO 110
3010 LET blocktype=INT (RND*7)
3020 IF blocktype=0 THEN LET b(2)=1: LET a(1)=1: LET a(2)=1:
LET a(3)=1
3030 IF blocktype=1 THEN LET a(1)=1: LET b(1)=1: LET b(2)=1:
LET b(3)=1
3035 IF blocktype=2 THEN LET a(3)=1: LET b(1)=1: LET b(2)=1:
LET b(3)=1
3040 IF blocktype=3 OR blocktype=3 THEN LET b(1)=1: LET
b(2)=1: LET a(1)=1: LET a(2)=1
3050 IF blocktype=4 THEN LET a(1)=1: LET b(1)=1: LET b(2)=1
3070 IF blocktype=5 THEN LET a(2)=1: LET b(1)=1: LET b(2)=1
3075 IF blocktype>5 THEN LET a(1)=1: LET b(1)=1: LET b(2)=1
3080 LET ypos=2: LET xpos=7+INT (RND*3)
3200 RETURN
3500 REM **** PRINT BLOCKS with alternate colour
3505 LET inkbl = INT (blocktype/2)+1
3510 FOR n =1 TO 3
3540 IF a(n)=1 THEN PRINT INK inkbl;AT ypos,xpos+(n-1);CHR$
(145)
3550 IF b(n)=1 THEN PRINT INK inkbl;AT ypos-1,xpos+(n-1);CHR$
(145)
3560 NEXT n
3570 RETURN
3600 REM **** CLEAR BLOCKS
3610 FOR n =1 TO 3
3620 IF a(n)=1 THEN PRINT PAPER 7;AT ypos-1,xpos+(n-
1)+offset;" "
```

```
3630 IF b(n)=1 THEN PRINT PAPER 7;AT ypos-2,xpos+(n-
1)+offset;" "
3660 NEXT n
3665 LET offset=0
3670 RETURN
3700 REM **** PRINT BLOCKS with standard colour
3710 FOR n =1 TO 3
3740 IF a(n)=1 THEN PRINT INK 1; PAPER 7;AT ypos,xpos+(n-
1);CHR$ (145)
3750 IF b(n)=1 THEN PRINT INK 1; PAPER 7;AT ypos-1,xpos+(n-
1);CHR$ (145)
3760 NEXT n
3770 RETURN
4000 REM *** CLEAR LINES
4010 LET count=0
4015 LET count2=0
4020 FOR n=7 TO 15:
4030 IF ATTR (ypos,n)<>56 THEN LET count=count+1
4035 IF ATTR (ypos-1,n)<>56 THEN LET count2=count2+1
4040 NEXT n
4050 IF count=9 THEN LET lines=lines+1
4055 IF count2=9 THEN LET lines=lines+1:
4056 IF count2<9 AND count < 9 THEN RETURN
4057 LET l$=CHR$ (145)+CHR$ (145)+CHR$ (145)+CHR$ (145)+CHR$
(145)+CHR$ (145)+CHR$ (145)+CHR$ (145)+CHR$ (145)
4058 LET score = score + (10*lines*(19-ypos))
4060 FOR n =0 TO 7
4070 BEEP .1,n
4080 IF count=9 THEN PRINT ;AT ypos,7; INK n;l$
4090 IF count2=9 THEN PRINT AT ypos-1,7; INK n;l$
4095 NEXT n:
4101 IF count=9 THEN LET cn=0
4102 IF count2=9 THEN LET  cn=1
4103 PRINT AT ypos-cn,7; INK 0; PAPER 7;"            "
4105 GO SUB 4700
```

```
4110 PRINT AT 5,20; PAPER 1; INK 7;lines;AT 8,20;"SCORE";AT
9,20;score
4120 RETURN
4500 REM *** SHIFT ALL DOWN 1 PLACE
4510 FOR n = ypos TO 4 STEP -1
4520 FOR m= 7 TO 15
4530 IF count2=9 AND ATTR (ypos-n-1,m)>56 THEN PRINT INK 0;
PAPER 7;AT ypos-1-n,m;" ";AT ypos-n+1,m;CHR$ (145)
4540 IF count=9 AND ATTR (ypos-n-1,m)>56 THEN PRINT INK 0;
PAPER 7;AT ypos-n,m;" ";AT ypos-n+1,m;CHR$ (145)
4590 NEXT m
4600 NEXT n
4610 RETURN
4700 REM *** ----------------------------SHIFT DOWN
4710 FOR n = ypos-cn TO 3 STEP -1
4720 FOR j = 7 TO 15
4725 LET att=ATTR (n,j)
4730 IF att<>56 THEN PRINT INK att-56; PAPER 7;AT n+1,j;CHR$
(145);AT n,j; INK 0; PAPER 7;" "
4740 NEXT j
4750 NEXT n
4760 RETURN
4800 IF blocktype > 5 THEN LET blocktype=5: BEEP .2,8: GO SUB
3600: LET a(1)=1: LET a(2)=0: GO SUB 3700: RETURN
4810 IF blocktype =5 THEN LET blocktype=6: BEEP .2,8: GO SUB
3600: LET a(2)=1: LET a(1)=0: GO SUB 3700: RETURN
4820 IF blocktype =2 THEN LET blocktype=1: BEEP .2,8: GO SUB
3600: LET a(3)=1: LET a(1)=0: GO SUB 3700: RETURN
4830 IF blocktype =1 THEN LET blocktype=2: BEEP .2,8: GO SUB
3600: LET a(1)=1: LET a(3)=0: GO SUB 3700: RETURN
4840 RETURN
5000 FOR n = 0 TO 23:
5010 READ dat
5020 POKE USR "a"+n,dat
5030 NEXT n
5050 RETURN
```

```
5100 DATA 85,162,85,168,21,170,69,170,255,129,189,165,165
,189,129,255
5110 DATA 255,145,145,145,255,133,133,255
```

What's New?

So the we start by building our game screen and limiting the movement within the Tetrix play area. The items will advance down the screen until they encounter the ground tiles or another block. Now the next item will start coming down one position at a time.

If the area below the block is occupied and the block cannot fit then the block will get stuck there and we are on the next block and so on.

Now that's all very easy, the hard part comes when we need to match and a line and bring down the rest of the blocks. This is done with an array, a loop and our friend the ATTR() function. As SCREEN$() will not work with UDGs and it does not distinguish colour attributes like ATTR() does.

```
4710 FOR n = ypos-cn TO 3 STEP -1
4720 FOR j = 7 TO 15
4725 LET att=ATTR (n,j)
4730 IF att<>56 THEN PRINT INK att-56; PAPER 7;AT n+1,j;CHR$
(145);AT n,j; INK 0; PAPER 7;" "
4740 NEXT j
4750 NEXT n
```

Above is some simple code that is used for shifting down the positions and colour attributes of the blocks above. Our Tetrix game is not perfect, but you could add more rotations on the shapes to improve it. I took a simple approach to try to keep it easy to understand and short enough to type in.

Suggestions for Extending (optional)

1]   *Add rotations on the shapes*
2]   *Try to add features to the game play*
3]   *Add more block graphic styles or a different theme*
       to the game

TYPE INVADERS

How about a game that tested your reflexes, spelling and how you coped under pressure. Well that's exactly what Type Invaders does. A game with a slight bit of educational content while still remaining at heart, a race against the clock. Compete against a friend or family member to see who can get the best score by remaining calm and composed.

Players: 1

Rules: Player types out the words as the attack the base on the right side of the screen.

Controls: Type out words, making an error will mean having to start the word again by hitting enter key. Also a fun game for kids – using smaller words.

```
  10 REM ******ZX Spectrum Code Club ********
  15 REM * TYPE INVADERS by Gary Plowman      *
  20 REM *********************************
  30 INK 7: PAPER 0: BORDER 4: CLS
  45 REM ****** Initialising variables
  50 PRINT AT 2,10; INK 7; BRIGHT 1; PAPER 0;"TYPE INVADERS":
PRINT AT 4,5;"Type Fast to Keep the Invaders":
  60 PRINT AT 4,5;"Mistakes cost Points!"
  80 PRINT AT 18,5; FLASH 1;"PRESS A KEY TO START": PAUSE 0:
 100 GO SUB 300: REM initialise
 130 GO SUB 1000: REM main loop for game
 200 GO TO 30:
 300 REM ***** SETUP
 310 LET lives=3: DIM a$(18,20): DIM x(18): DIM y(18): LET
score=0: LET misses=0: LET t$="": LET limit=3: LET lmt=0
```

```
 320 RESTORE 340
 305 RANDOMIZE
 330 FOR n=1 TO 18:
 340 READ d$
 350 LET a$(n)=d$: LET y(n)=INT (RND*18)+1
 370 NEXT n
 390 RETURN
1000 CLS : REM ******* MAIN GAME
1010 FOR n = 1 TO 19
1020 PRINT AT n,30; PAPER 6; INK RND*5;CHR$ (139);CHR$ (139)
1030 NEXT n
1031 FOR n = 1 TO 170
1032 PLOT INK RND*6;INT (RND*210),n
1036 NEXT n
1038 PRINT AT 0,0;"        ** TYPE INVADERS **"
1040 LET i$=INKEY$
1045 LET lmt=0
1050 FOR n = 1 TO 18:
1060 IF x(n)>0 THEN PRINT AT y(n),x(n);" ";a$(n): LET
lmt=lmt+1: LET x(n)=x(n)+.5
1080 IF x(n)=30 THEN GO SUB 2000:
1070 IF i$="" THEN LET i$=INKEY$
1090 NEXT n
1100 IF lmt<limit THEN LET test=INT (RND*17)+1
1110 IF x(test)=0 THEN LET x(test)=1: LET y(test)=test:
1120 IF i$="" THEN LET i$=INKEY$:
1130 IF i$=CHR$ (13) THEN BEEP .05,4: GO SUB 1500: REM ***
check for match
1200 IF i$<"a" AND i$>"z" THEN GO TO 1040
1205 IF i$<>"" THEN BEEP .02,10
1210 LET t$=t$+i$
1220 PRINT AT 20,0; PAPER 7; INK 2;t$
1230 PRINT AT 20,13; INK 7; BRIGHT 1;"Score:";score;"
Misses:";misses
1400 GO TO 1040:
1500 REM **** Checking for a hit
```

```
1510 LET r$="": LET s$="": LET sc=LEN t$*10
1520 FOR m=1 TO 18
1522 FOR p=1 TO 20-LEN t$
1523 LET t$=t$+" "
1525 NEXT p
1530 IF t$=a$(m) THEN PRINT AT y(m),x(m); PAPER 6; INK
2;"***": LET x(m)=0: LET score=score+sc: LET misses=misses-1:
BEEP .1,14: GO TO 1550
1540 NEXT m
1550 LET t$="": PRINT AT 20,0;"                    ": LET
i$="": LET misses=misses+1
1600 RETURN
2000 REM ***** GAME OVER
2010 PRINT AT 18,13; INK 2;"** BASE DESTROYED **"
2020 PRINT AT 10,10; FLASH 1;"PRESS TO RESTART"
2030 IF INKEY$="" THEN GO TO 2030
2050 GO TO 100
3000 DATA "fun","fast","type","good","shoot","bang"
3010 DATA "planets","invaders","cosmic","sinclair",
"spectrum","coding"
3020 DATA "missedme","comingtogetu","fireatwill",
"launchmissile","blazingthruster","supercharged"
```

What's New?

As before we are using INKEY$ to capture key presses but this time we are simulating text entry and allowing for the Enter key (CHR$(13)) to finish the entry sequence.

```
1120 IF i$="" THEN LET i$=INKEY$:
1130 IF i$=CHR$ (13) THEN BEEP .05,4: GO SUB 1500: REM ***
check for match
```

Another new command introduced here is LEN. This just simply returns a value for the length of the string you wish to query.

We also used DATA to store our string values for our words. Below is the code used to READ in those words and place them randomly on your screen.

```
330 FOR n=1 TO 18:
 340 READ d$
 350 LET a$(n)=d$: LET y(n)=INT (RND*18)+1
 370 NEXT n
```

Each string of the array is associated with an array value, y() for the y-axis screen position. Lines 1520 to 1540 test your answer and fill out your string with the blank spaces that Sinclair BASIC needs when working with string arrays. Sinclair BASIC string arrays are always fixed in length, and pad out each value with spaces.

Suggestions for Extending (optional)

1]   Add more words or change the existing words
2]   Increase speed of the game over the levels
3]   Randomise the speed of the words so that some words are
      faster than others and need to be entered first

MINIPONG

Based on another classic that appeared in the Arcades and at home on the consoles such as the Atari 2600. Who doesn't remember the unforgettable sound of the square ball missing your bat. Pong, the original arcade version, was made up entirely of discrete logic chips (no CPU) and was a phenomenon across the world. This is a short simple version of how to do a pong clone.

Players: 1

Rules: Hit the ball to other computer. Avoid missing to win!

Controls: q = up, a = down

```
  10 REM ******ZX Spectrum Code Club *******
  15 REM * MINIPONG by Gary Plowman         *
  20 REM **************2015******************
  30 INK 7: PAPER 0: BORDER 0: CLS
  45 REM ****** Initialising variables
  50 PRINT AT 2,10; INK 7; BRIGHT 1; PAPER 2;"MINI PONG":
PAUSE 0
  35 LET lives=3
 100 GO SUB 300: REM initialise
 120 GO SUB 500: REM menu
 130 GO SUB 1000: REM main loop for game
 200 GO TO 30
 300 LET ply=2: LET win=0: DIM a(9,2): DIM d(30): LET lvl=1:
LET posy=30: LET y=10: LET y2=10: LET frm=0: LET score=0: LET
score2=0: LET time=0: LET mov=11: LET ball=0: LET vx=0: LET
vy=0: LET p$=CHR$ (143)
```

```
 400 RETURN
 500 CLS
 510 LET w$=CHR$ (140)
 520 FOR n = 0 TO 31
 530 PRINT INK 7;AT 1,n;w$;AT 21,n;w$
 540 NEXT n
 542 LET w$=CHR$ (136)
 545 FOR n = 2 TO 20 STEP 2
 546 PRINT INK 7; AT n,15;w$
 549 NEXT n
 550 RETURN
1000 IF score=10 OR score2=10 THEN PRINT AT 10,10; FLASH 1;"G
A M E  O V E R";AT 12,10;"RESTARTING": PAUSE 0: GO TO 30: REM
Main Loop
1002 LET bx=10: LET by=10
1003 PRINT AT 0,10;score;AT 0,18;score2
1005 PRINT AT y-1,2;" ";AT y,2;p$;AT y+1,2;p$;AT y+2,2;" "
1008 PRINT AT y2-1,27;" ";AT y2,27;p$;AT y2+1,27;p$;AT
y2+2,27;" "
1010 LET i$=INKEY$: LET kemp=IN 31
1120 IF (i$="q" OR kemp=8) AND y>3 THEN LET y=y-1
1130 IF (i$="a" OR kemp=4) AND y<18 THEN LET y=y+1
1150 GO SUB 2000: REM ************Move Ball
1180 GO SUB 2500: REM ************Player 2 AI
1400 GO TO 1005
2000 REM *** Move Ball
2010 IF vx=0 AND vy=0 THEN LET vx=-1: LET vy=(RND*2)-(RND*2):
BEEP .1,4
2030 PRINT AT by,bx;" "
2038 LET collide = ABS (by-y): LET collide2 = ABS (by-y2)
2040 IF by+vy>19 THEN LET vy=-1*(vy)
2050 IF by+vy<3 THEN LET vy=-1*(vy)
2055 IF bx+vx>27 AND collide2>1 THEN LET score=score+1: LET
vx=0: LET vy=0: BEEP 1,0: GO TO 1000
2060 IF bx+vx<3 AND ABS collide>1 THEN LET score2=score2+1:
BEEP 1,0: GO TO 1000
```

```
2065 IF bx+vx>27 AND collide2<1 THEN LET vx=-1*(vx): LET
vy=(RND*3)-(RND*3): BEEP .2,4
2070 IF bx+vx<3 AND collide<1 THEN LET vx=-1*(vx): LET
vy=(RND*3)-(RND*3): BEEP .2,4
2080 LET bx=bx+vx: LET by=by+vy:
2090 PRINT AT by,bx;p$
2100 RETURN
2500 REM **** PLAYER 2 movement
2510 IF y2>by+vy AND bx>9 THEN LET y2=y2-.8
2520 IF y2<by+vy AND bx>9 THEN LET y2=y2+.8
2550 RETURN
```

What's New?

Some basic movement AI for the opponent. Simple bouncing achieved using a reversal of the horizontal or vertical direction value. To increase the difficulty you can increase the player 2 speed settings.

```
2500 REM **** PLAYER 2 movement
2510 IF y2>by+vy AND bx>9 THEN LET y2=y2-.8
2520 IF y2<by+vy AND bx>9 THEN LET y2=y2+.8
```

Suggestions for Extending (optional)

1] Increase difficulty
2] Add obstacles to vary the bouncing
3] Make two player with one player using the joystick
4] Add additional colour theme options

TAKEAWAY TED

> *Ted must manage his Takeaway shop well or risk losing customers and money.*
> *Also his missus will give him an ear-bashing if he messes it up too much. Ted must*
> *feed the customers with the correct orders to bring in the moolah! If a food queue*
> *is fully used then Ted will save money on the running costs. If he gives the*
> *customer the wrong food...Uh oh!*

Players: 1

Rules: Start your queue and as the customers come into your chip shop you have
to match their orders with what's in your queue.

Letters on screen: C = Chips, B = Burger, F = Fish, P = Pizza and K = Kebab

Match the orders to your customer queue. 'K' key will generate a new list of
food items but it will cost money. Using all available items gets you a free
list of food to serve. Give a wrong order to a customer and you lose some
of your money. The shop costs money to run so try to make enough to keep
it open.

Controls: k = make up to 5 food items. Selecting food: keys a, b, c, d or e to select
food. Keys 1 – 8 to give item to customers.

```
10 REM ******ZX Spectrum Code Club *******
15 REM * TAKEAWAY TED (Chip Shop Sim)    *
20 REM ******** Gary Plowman 2015 ********
30 INK 2: PAPER 0: BORDER 0: CLS
45 REM ****** Initialising variables
50 PRINT AT 1,8;"TAKEAWAY TED": PAUSE 0
```

```
  35 DIM p(2): DIM l(10): DIM c(8): LET cash=30: LET
speed=100: DIM c$(8): LET cust=0: DIM q$(5): LET k$="CBFPK":
LET take = 0: LET timer=20: LET score=0
 100 GO SUB 300: REM initialise and start game
 130 GO SUB 1000: REM main loop for game
 200 GO TO 30
 300 REM *** DRAW SCREEN
 310 CLS
 320 INK 6: PLOT 20,150: DRAW 0,-100: DRAW 200,0: DRAW 0,100:
PLOT 30,70: DRAW 180,0: DRAW 0,80: PLOT 30,70: DRAW 0,80
 325 INK 4: PLOT 100,104: DRAW 0,15: DRAW 15,0: DRAW 0,-15:
DRAW -15,0: PLOT 105,114: DRAW 0,-5: PLOT 110,114: DRAW 0,-5
 326 INK 6: PLOT 107,102: DRAW 0,-7: DRAW -5,0
 327 PLOT 112,102: DRAW 0,-9: DRAW -5,0:
 330 PRINT AT 20,12; PAPER 2; INK 7;"Door":
 340 INK 3: PRINT AT 20,0; PAPER 6;"Ted's Chips";AT 20,17;"
Take Away "
 350 PRINT AT 14,19;" Counter"
 360 PRINT AT 14,3;"12345678":
 370 INK 4: PRINT AT 0,10;"CASH: $";cash; "  Sc:"; score
 380 FOR n = 1 TO 5: PRINT AT 2+n,4; INK 6;CHR$ (64+n): NEXT n
 390 REM ** draw more...
 400 INK 5: PLOT 120,130: DRAW -34,0:
 410 PLOT 140,130: DRAW 0,30: FOR n = 10 TO 30 STEP 4: PLOT
137,130+n: DRAW 7,0: NEXT n
 420 PRINT AT 4,11;"Oven";AT 2,19;"Kebab";AT 2,0; BRIGHT
1;"K=New Food"
 430 PRINT INK 6;AT 6,18;"_menu__"; BRIGHT 1;AT 7,17;"Chips
$2";AT 8,17;"Burger $3";AT 9,17;"Fish   $5";AT 10,17;"Pizza
$8";AT 11,17;"Kebab  $4"
 500 RETURN
1000 LET a$=INKEY$: LET timer=timer-1
1002 IF timer<0 AND INT (RND*4)>2 THEN LET c$(INT (RND*8)+1)="
"
1005 IF timer<0 THEN LET timer=10: LET cash=cash-1
1008 IF a$="" THEN GO TO 3800
```

```
1110 IF a$="k" THEN GO SUB 4200: GO SUB 4100
1120 IF a$="a" THEN LET take=1: PRINT AT 3,7;"-": BEEP .3,5
1130 IF a$="b" THEN LET take=2: PRINT AT 4,7;"-": BEEP .3,5
1140 IF a$="c" THEN LET take=3: PRINT AT 5,7;"-": BEEP .3,5
1150 IF a$="d" THEN LET take=4: PRINT AT 6,7;"-": BEEP .3,5
1160 IF a$="e" THEN LET take=5: PRINT AT 7,7;"-": BEEP .3,5:
1170 IF take>0 AND a$>="1" AND a$<="8" THEN GO SUB 4700: GO
SUB 4100
3800 GO SUB 4300
3810 GO SUB 4600
3900 GO TO 1000
4100 REM *** PRINT KITCHEN QUEUE
4110 INK 2: FOR n = 1 TO 5
4120 PRINT AT 2+n,6;q$(n);" "
4130 NEXT n
4150 RETURN
4200 REM *** ADD TO QUEUE
4205 LET cash = cash - 5
4206 RANDOMIZE
4208 FOR n = 1 TO 8
4210 LET r =INT (RND*10): LET qpos =INT (RND*5)+1
4220 IF r = 1 OR r=6 THEN LET q$(qpos)="B"
4230 IF r = 2 OR r=7 THEN LET q$(qpos)="C"
4240 IF r = 3 THEN LET q$(qpos)="F"
4250 IF r = 4 THEN LET q$(qpos)="K"
4252 IF r = 5 THEN LET q$(qpos)="P"
4255 BEEP .02,qpos
4260 NEXT n
4290 RETURN
4300 REM **** RECALC SCREEN
4310 INK 4: PRINT AT 0,10;"CASH: $";cash;"   ";" Sc:";score
4320 FOR n = 1 TO 8
4330 PRINT BRIGHT 1;AT 16,2+n;c$(n)
4340 NEXT n
4400 RETURN
```

```
4600 REM **** NEW CUSTOMER?
4610 RANDOMIZE : LET r =INT (RND*20)
4620 LET p =INT (RND*8)+1
4630 LET order=INT (RND*5)+1
4640 IF r>4 THEN RETURN
4650 IF c$(p)=" " THEN LET c$(p)=k$(order)
4690 RETURN
4700 REM **** GIVE OUT ORDER
4705 BEEP .2,11
4710 LET qpos =VAL a$
4720 IF q$(take)="C" THEN LET price=2
4730 IF q$(take)="B" THEN LET price=3
4740 IF q$(take)="P" THEN LET price=8
4750 IF q$(take)="F" THEN LET price=5
4760 IF q$(take)="K" THEN LET price=4
4765 IF c$(qpos)<>q$(take) THEN GO TO 4820
4770 IF c$(qpos)=q$(take) AND q$(take)<>" " THEN LET cash =
cash + price: LET c$(qpos)=" ": LET q$(take)="-": LET take=0:
LET score=score+1
4775 LET count=0
4780 FOR n = 1 TO 5
4785 IF q$(n)=" " OR q$(n)="-" THEN LET count=count+1
4790 NEXT n
4800 IF count=5 THEN LET cash=cash+5: GO SUB 4200
4810 RETURN
4820 LET cash = cash - 10: LET c$(qpos)=" ": LET q$(take)="-":
LET take=0
4900 RETURN
```

What's New?

Wackiness galore and who doesn't love a bag of chips! The game is a queue based game which needs quick reflexes to get your goods out the door in the hands of your customers. This one might make your brain hurt.

We created graphics with PLOTs and DRAWs rather than UDGs here as there was no screen action to be concerned with.

```
326 INK 6: PLOT 107,102: DRAW 0,-7: DRAW -5,0
```

DRAW has a third parameter which is used for providing the angle of the line. We did not use it – but it is handy to know it's there in case you plan to try something with it.

> ### *Suggestions for Extending (optional)*
>
> 1]   *Increase difficulty*
> 2]   *Add more items or change the theme*
> 3]   *Turn the wackiness up to 11*

C5 SOLAR RACE

Sir Clive Sinclair has successfully funded his Kickstarter to build 4 Solar C5s for use in his annual Sinclair C5 Solar Derby Race. The 4 contenders will race over 200m to win the coveted trophy which will be presented by Sir Clive himself. The trophy is constructed entirely from pre-used white ZX80 plastic casings.

Players: 2

Rules: Up to Four players (sort of), you press down the number of your C5 Car to increase speed but if you run out of power you stall and need to allow the sun to regenerate your battery.

Controls: Keys 1 to 4.

```
  10 REM *****************
  20 REM *  C5 Solar Race *
  30 REM *  Gary Plowman  *
  40 REM *****************
 100 PAPER 7: INK 0: BORDER 7: BRIGHT 1: CLS :
 140 GO SUB 300: REM setup game
 150 GO SUB 1000: REM draw screen
 160 GO SUB 2000: REM main loop:
 300 LET a$=CHR$  136: LET b$=CHR$ 139+CHR$ 142+CHR$ 140+CHR$
134: LET c$=CHR$ 142+CHR$  140+CHR$  140+CHR$ 140+CHR$ 138:
 310 LET s$=CHR$  143+CHR$ 143: LET t$=CHR$  143+CHR$ 143+CHR$
143+CHR$ 143: DIM p(4): DIM x(4): LET dist=0
 320 FOR n =1 TO 4: LET p(n)=10: LET x(n)=1: NEXT n
 330 LET ply=1: LET l$="": LET q$="": LET redraw=0
```

```
 340 FOR n=1 TO 31: LET l$=l$+CHR$  132: LET q$=q$+CHR$ 136:
NEXT n:
1000 PRINT INK 6;AT 0,24;s$;AT 1,23;t$;AT 2,23;t$;AT
3,23;t$;AT 4,24;s$
1010 FOR n = 5 TO 17: PRINT AT n,0; INK 7; PAPER 0;"
": NEXT n
1020 FOR n = 1 TO 4
1050 PRINT PAPER 0; INK 7;AT n*3+2,x(n);a$;AT n*3+3,x(n);b$;AT
n*3+4,x(n);c$;AT n*3+2,x(n); INK n+1;CHR$ 143
1060 NEXT n
1080 PRINT AT 0,0;"Players 1 - 4 for Boost";AT 4,0;"200m
Race!"
1090 RANDOMIZE
1100 LET i$=INKEY$:
1105 PRINT AT 1,0;dist;"m": LET dist=dist+1
1110 GO SUB 2000: REM anim screen
1115 GO SUB 2500: REM accelerate
1118 IF dist>200 THEN GO SUB 5000
1120 IF i$<"1" OR i$>"4" THEN GO TO 1100
1130 LET v=VAL i$
1140 IF p(v)>2 THEN LET p(v)=p(v)-INT (RND*3): LET
x(v)=x(v)+.5: BEEP .01,5
1150 IF p(v)<2 THEN LET x(v)=x(v)-2: LET p(v)=2: BEEP .01,-5:
1180 GO SUB 3500
1190 GO SUB 3000
1900 GO TO 1100
2000 REM *** Screen anim
2010 IF ATTR (18,0)<69 THEN  PRINT AT 18,0; INK 5; PAPER 0;l$:
RETURN
2010 PRINT AT 18,0; INK 0; PAPER 0;" "; INK 5;q$
2020 FOR n = 1 TO 4
2030 IF p(n)<9 THEN LET p(n)=p(n)+.4
2040 NEXT n
2100 RETURN
2500 REM *** Acc
2510 LET choose=INT (RND*4)+1
```

```
2520 LET x(choose)=x(choose)+RND*2
2530 LET v=choose: GO SUB 3500
2570 RETURN
3000 REM *** power bar
3005 PRINT AT 20,0; INK 2;"P";v
3010 FOR n = 1 TO p(v): PRINT AT 20,n+3; INK 2;CHR$ 138;"
": NEXT n
3020 RETURN
3500 REM *** ReDraw C5 Buggy
3510 IF x(1)>25 OR x(2)>25 OR x(3)>25 OR x(4)>25 THEN GO SUB
3800: GO SUB 3700: REM ** Scroll Screen
3550 LET pos=v*3+2:
3560 PRINT PAPER 0; INK 7;AT pos,x(v)-2;"   ";AT pos+1,x(v)-2;"
";AT pos+2,x(v)-2;"   "
3570 PRINT PAPER 0; INK 7;AT v*3+2,x(v);a$;AT v*3+3,x(v);b$;AT
v*3+4,x(v);c$;AT v*3+2,x(v); INK v+1;CHR$ 143:
3600 RETURN
3700 REM *** Scroll
3710 FOR n =1 TO 4: LET x(n)=x(n)-10
3720 IF x(n)<0 THEN LET x(n)=2
3730 NEXT n
3760 RETURN
3800 REM *** redraw
3810 FOR n =1 TO 4
3820 PRINT PAPER 0; INK 7;AT n*3+2,x(n)-2;"        ";AT
n*3+3,x(n)-2;"        ";AT n*3+4,x(n)-2;"        "
3830 IF x(n)<2 THEN LET x(n)=2
3840 NEXT n
3850 RETURN
5000 REM *** Declare winner
5010 LET win=0: LET winner=0
5020 FOR n =1 TO 4
5030 IF x(n)> win THEN LET win=x(n): LET winner=n
5040 NEXT n
5050 PRINT AT 10,10;"WINNER IS"
```

```
5060 PRINT AT 12,10;"Player ";winner: BEEP 2,8: PAUSE 0: GO TO
100
5070 RETURN
```

Prototyping a game

Using really basic graphics for a game idea is a good way to test the idea before investing too much time into doing a lot of coding. BASIC is really fun for prototyping with. A prototype is like a crude demo model of something. Next time you think of a game idea, try to make it in BASIC and see if its fun. If it is then you probably have a good case to build your idea into a full game!

Simple Block Graphics

Block graphics are retro and the Minecraft look is very popular. You can use the Spectrum graphics characters to create simple graphics for your games – saving you from having to create unnecessary UDGs for simple shapes.

Suggestions for Extending (optional)

1]   *More C5's*
2]   *Use your imagination and go wild*

PENALTY SHOOTOUT

Everyone loves a good Penalty Shootout. So you can code in your own 2 player version here. Timing is everything in this little fun game. Hopefully you won't fall out with any friends while playing it. Have a good time and don't spill your tea in frustration.

Players: 2

Rules: Player 1 in Blue, Player 2 in Red. Taking turns and first to 5 wins proving the opponent is at least 2 points behind. Shooter takes his shot then the player in goal gets a chance to save it.

Controls: S = Shoot at goal (try not to go wide!), G = Goalkeeper makes a save attempt.

```
  10 REM ******ZX Spectrum Code Club *******
  15 REM * PENALTY SHOOTOUT - G Plowman      *
  20 REM ********************************
  30 INK 1: PAPER 4: BORDER 4: CLS
  45 REM ****** Initialising variables
  50 PRINT AT 1,5; INK 7; BRIGHT 1; PAPER 2;"PENALTY
SHOOTOUT": PAUSE 0
  35 LET lives=3: LET dice=0: LET ply=1: DIM p(2): DIM l(10):
DIM c(2): LET miss=0
 100 GO SUB 300: REM initialise
 120 GO SUB 500: REM menu
 130 GO SUB 1000: REM main loop for game
 200 GO TO 30
 300 PRINT AT 2,8; INK 1; BRIGHT 1;"0123456789";AT 10,8; INK
1; BRIGHT 1;"0123456789":
```

```
 320 FOR n = 1 TO 3: PRINT AT 3+n,0; INK n;"OoOoOooOo";AT
3+n,10; PAPER 7;"        "; PAPER 4; INK n+1;" OoOoOooOo": NEXT
n
 330 PRINT AT 6,0; PAPER 2;"==========";AT 6,16;"=========="
 340 PLOT 80,190-(6*8): DRAW 10,-14: PLOT 80+6*8,190-(6*8):
DRAW -10,-14
1000 PRINT AT 18,10;"                  ": FOR n = 1 TO INT
(RND*15)+4: BEEP .1,n: NEXT n
1001 IF ply=1 THEN PRINT AT 16,0;"PLAYER 1 to (s)hoot (score
is ";p(1);")"
1002 IF ply=2 THEN PRINT AT 16,0;"PLAYER 2 to (s)hoot (score
is ";p(2);")"
1003 PRINT AT 20,0; PAPER 7;"Ply 1:";p(1);"   Ply 2:";p(2):
1005 BEEP .3,10: LET inkc = 1: IF ply=2 THEN LET inkc=2:
1006 PRINT INK inkc; AT 10,6;CHR$ (139);AT 11,5;CHR$
(137);CHR$ (143);CHR$ (134);AT 12,6;CHR$ (142)
1010 FOR n = 1 TO 10
1020 LET i$=INKEY$
1030 PRINT AT 11,8+(n-2); INK 6;" ";CHR$ (143);" "
1040 IF i$="s" THEN GO TO 1100
1045 NEXT n: PRINT AT 11,16;"   "
1050 GO TO 1010
1090 BEEP .3,10
1100 IF ply=1 THEN PRINT AT 16,0; INK 2;"PLAYER 2 to save
(g)oal            "
1102 IF ply=2 THEN PRINT AT 16,0; INK 1;"PLAYER 1 to save
(g)aol            "
1110 FOR m = 1 TO 10
1120 LET i$=INKEY$
1130 PRINT AT 3,8+(m-2); INK 6;" ";CHR$ (143);" "
1140 IF i$="g" THEN GO TO 1200
1145 NEXT m: PRINT AT 3,16;"   "
1150 GO TO 1110
1200 LET c(ply) = c(ply) + 1 : LET miss=0
1210 IF n=m THEN PRINT AT 18,10;"S A V E D!": LET miss=1:
```

```
1220 IF n<>m OR (n<3 OR n>7) THEN PRINT AT 18,10;"Wide!!
": LET miss=1
1225 IF n<>m AND (n>2 AND n<8) THEN PRINT AT 18,10; INK 2;"G O
A L !!! ": LET miss=0
1230 REM IF ply =1 AND miss=1
1240 IF ply =1 AND miss=0 THEN LET p(ply)=p(ply)+1: BEEP 1,14
1250 REM IF ply =2 AND miss=1 THEN LET l(c(ply))=0
1260 IF ply =2 AND miss=0 THEN LET p(ply)=p(ply)+1: BEEP 1,14
1270 IF miss=1 THEN BEEP 1,-1
1275 IF miss=9 THEN BEEP 1,-1
1276 PRINT AT 11,9;"          ";AT 3,9;"            "
1280 IF ply=1 THEN LET ply=2: GO SUB 2000
1290 IF ply=2 THEN LET ply=1: GO SUB 2000
1300 GO TO 1000:
2000 REM ** CHECK FOR WINNER
2010 IF p(1)<5 AND p(2)<5 THEN GO TO 1000
2020 IF p(1)>=5 AND p(1)-p(2)>=2 THEN LET win=1: GO SUB 3000
2030 IF p(2)>=5 AND p(2)-p(1)>=2 THEN LET win=2: GO SUB 3000
2050 RETURN
3000 REM *** WINNER
3010 PRINT AT 10,10; FLASH 1;"WINNER IS PLAYER ";win:
3020 PAUSE 0: PAUSE 0: CLS
3030 BEEP 2,10
3050 GO TO 45
```

Suggestions for Extending (optional)

1]   *Add better graphics*
2]   *Change around completely and make your own footy game*
    with the penalty part becoming the scoring scene for the
    game

BILLY BOB'S GOLD

> *This little game is a mash-up of a few games. Part Hungry Horace, part Pac-man, part a race against the clock. Your Claim to your mine is under threat from three bad outlaws. They are looking to find you and put you out of your mine so they can keep all the gold.*

Players: 1

Rules: Collect the Gold from Billy Bob's mine while avoiding the Outlaws. Be careful not to run down your timer.

Controls: q = up, a = down, o = left, p = right. Also the joystick if connected as a Kempston.

```
  10 REM ********** ZX Code Club **********
  20 REM * Billy Bob's Gold - Gary Plowman *
  25 REM ********************************
  30 INK 6: PAPER 0: BORDER 0: BRIGHT 1: CLS
  40 GO SUB 6000
  50 PRINT AT 2,6; INK 7; BRIGHT 1; PAPER 0;"BILLY BOB'S
GOLD": PRINT AT 4,5;""
  60 PRINT AT 6,0;"Collect gold beware the outlaws";AT
8,0;"Gold nuggets slow the Timer!"
  80 PRINT AT 18,5; FLASH 1;"PRESS A KEY TO START": PAUSE 0:
CLS : RANDOMIZE : INK 0
 110 GO SUB 300: REM initialise:
 130 GO SUB 1000: REM draw screen
 140 GO SUB 2000: REM main loop
 300 REM *******
 305 LET score=0: LET maxgold=0
```

```
 310 LET x= 7: LET y=17: LET vy=0: LET vx=0: LET timer=99
 320 LET ex1=2: LET ex2 = 22: LET e$=".": LET f$=".": LET
ey1=4: LET ey2=4
 330 LET vx1=0: LET vx2=0: LET vy1=0: LET vy2=0: LET vx3=0:
LET vy3=0: LET ey3=18: LET ex3=22: LET h$="."
 340 LET r3=0
 400 RETURN
1000 REM ****** Screen
1010 CLS : INK 7: PAPER 0: PRINT INK 4;AT 0,0;"      Billy
Bob's Gold"
1015 INK 0
1020 PRINT AT 03,0;"MMMMMMMMMMMMMMMMMMMMMMMM"
1030 PRINT AT 04,0;"M                      M"
1040 PRINT AT 05,0;"M  MMMMMMM  M  MMMMMM  M"
1050 PRINT AT 06,0;"M          M  M  M     M"
1060 PRINT AT 07,0;"M  M MMMM M  M  M MM MM  M"
1070 PRINT AT 08,0;"M  M              MM   M"
1080 PRINT AT 09,0;"M  MMMMMMM  M  MMMM MM  M"
1090 PRINT AT 10,0;"M          M     M     M"
1100 PRINT AT 11,0;"MMMM      M    MMM    MMMM"
1110 PRINT AT 12,0;"M                    M  M"
1115 PRINT AT 13,0;"M  MMMM MMM  M  MMMMMM  M"
1120 PRINT AT 14,0;"M                      M"
1125 PRINT AT 15,0;"MM MMMMMMM  M  MMMMMM MM"
1130 PRINT AT 16,0;"M              M        M"
1140 PRINT AT 17,0;"M  MMMMMMM  M  MMM MMM  M"
1145 PRINT AT 18,0;"M                      M"
1150 PRINT AT 19,0;"MMMMMMMMMMMMMMMMMMMMMMMM"
1155 INK 7
1160 FOR n=3 TO 19
1170 FOR m = 0 TO 25
1180 IF SCREEN$ (n,m)="M" THEN PRINT AT n,m; PAPER 1; INK
1;"M"
1185 IF SCREEN$ (n,m)=" " THEN PRINT AT n,m; INK 6;"."
1190 NEXT m: NEXT n
2000 REM GAME LOOP ****************************************
```

```
2010 LET i$=INKEY$: LET j=IN 31
2110 IF (i$="q" OR j=8) THEN LET vy=-1: LET vx=0
2120 IF (i$="a" OR j=4) THEN LET vy=1: LET vx=0
2130 IF (i$="o" OR j=1) THEN LET vx=-1: LET vy=0
2140 IF (i$="p" OR j=2) THEN LET vx=1: LET vy=0
2190 IF SCREEN$ (y+vy,x+vx)<>"M" THEN PRINT AT y,x;" ": LET
x=x+vx: LET y=y+vy
2195 LET y$=SCREEN$ (y,x)
2200 IF y$="." THEN LET score= score +1: LET timer=timer+1:
LET maxgold=maxgold+1: BEEP .01,8
2240 IF timer> 160 THEN LET timer=160:
2290 PRINT AT y,x;CHR$ (144);AT 20,18;"Clock:";timer;" ";AT
2,0; INK 6;"Score:";score
2300 LET timer=timer-1
2310 IF timer <= 0 THEN PRINT AT 10,10;"GAME OVER";AT
12,10;"SCORE WAS ";score: BEEP 2,10: CLS : GO TO 50
2400 IF maxgold=score THEN LET maxgold=maxgold*2: PRINT AT
10,10;"NEXT LEVEL": BEEP 1,8: BEEP .5,10: GO SUB 310: GO TO
130
2420 PRINT AT ey1,ex1; INK 6;CHR$ (145);AT ey2,ex2; INK 5;CHR$
(145);AT ey3,ex3; INK 4;CHR$ (145)
2430 GO SUB 4000:
3000 GO TO 2000
3010 REM
****************************************************************
4000 REM **** MOVE ENEMIES
4010 LET r1=0: LET r2=0: LET r3=0: RANDOMIZE
4020 IF (vx1=0 AND vy1=0) OR (ex1=11 OR ex1=14) THEN LET
r1=INT (RND*4)+1
4025 IF (vx2=0 AND vy2=0) OR (ex2=11 OR ex2=14) THEN LET
r2=INT (RND*4)+1
4030 IF (vx3=0 AND vy3=0) OR (ex3=11 OR ex3=14) THEN LET
r3=INT (RND*4)+1:
4040 REM IF ABS (vy-vy1)<4 AND ABS (vy-vy1)<4 THEN LET vx1=vx
AND vy1=vy
4060 IF vy1=0 AND r1=1 THEN LET vx1 =-1: GO TO 4080
```

```
4065 IF vy1=0 AND r1=2 THEN LET vx1 =1: GO TO 4080
4070 IF vy1=0 AND r1=3 THEN LET vy1 =-1: GO TO 4080
4075 IF vy1=0 AND r1=4 THEN LET vy1 =1
4080 IF vy2=0 AND r2=1 THEN LET vx2 =-1: GO TO 4120
4095 IF vy2=0 AND r2=2 THEN LET vx2 =1: GO TO 4120
4100 IF vy2=0 AND r2=3 THEN LET vy2 =-1: GO TO 4120
4110 IF vy2=0 AND r2=4 THEN LET vy2 =1
4120 IF vy3=0 AND r3=1 THEN LET vx3 =-1: GO TO 4200
4135 IF vy3=0 AND r3=2 THEN LET vx3 =1: GO TO 4200
4140 IF vy3=0 AND r3=3 THEN LET vy3 =-1: GO TO 4200
4150 IF vy3=0 AND r3=4 THEN LET vy3 =1
4200 REM *** move ::
4210 PRINT INK 6; AT ey1,ex1;e$;AT ey2,ex2;f$;AT ey3,ex3;h$:
4215 IF SCREEN$ (ey1+vy1,ex1+vx1)="M" THEN LET vy1=0: LET
vx1=0
4216 IF SCREEN$ (ey2+vy2,ex2+vx2)="M" THEN LET vy2=0: LET
vx2=0
4218 IF SCREEN$ (ey3+vy3,ex3+vx3)="M" THEN LET vy3=0: LET
vx3=0:
4220 LET ex1 = ex1 + vx1: LET ey1=ey1+vy1
4230 LET ex2 = ex2 + vx2: LET ey2=ey2+vy2
4232 LET ex3 = ex3 + vx3: LET ey3=ey3+vy3
4235 LET e$=SCREEN$ (ey1,ex1): LET f$=SCREEN$ (ey2,ex2): LET
h$=SCREEN$ (ey3,ex3)
4240 PRINT AT ey1,ex1; INK 6;CHR$ (145);AT ey2,ex2; INK 5;CHR$
(145);AT ey3,ex3; INK 4;CHR$ (145)
4250 IF ABS (x-ex1)<2 AND ABS (y-ey1)<2 THEN GO SUB 4600
4260 IF ABS (x-ex2)<2 AND ABS (y-ey2)<2 THEN GO SUB 4600
4270 IF ABS (x-ex3)<2 AND ABS (y-ey3)<2 THEN GO SUB 4600
4410 RETURN
4600 REM ***** GAME OVER
4610 PRINT AT 10,10;"GAME OVER";AT 12,10;"SCORE WAS ";score
4620 FOR n = 1 TO 10: BEEP n/10,n: NEXT n
4630 CLS
4640 GO TO 50
4650 RETURN
```

```
5999 REM **** GRAPHICS
6000 FOR n = 0 TO 15
6010 READ dat
6020 POKE USR "a"+n,dat
6030 NEXT n
6040 RETURN
6100 DATA  24,60,24,27,15,11,24,60,24,126,36,153,126, 24,36,36
```

What's New?

Look we have used ABS once again to test for collision with baddies.

```
4250 IF ABS (x-ex1)<2 AND ABS (y-ey1)<2 THEN GO SUB 4600
```

Also in order to mix up the baddie movement we added very basic AI to change direction of the baddie randomly.

```
4020 IF (vx1=0 AND vy1=0) OR (ex1=11 OR ex1=14) THEN LET
r1=INT (RND*4)+1
```

Maze Games

Who doesn't love maze games! In the 1980s everyone went crazy for a dot munching Icon. So here we have added 3 baddies with basic rudimentary AI (random) and a few hacks to make the baddies go down the centre part of the screen maze. Lots can be done with this, our final game in this book.

Suggestions for Extending (optional)
1]   *Increase difficulty*
2]   *Add another baddie*
3]   *Change around and make your own maze chaser!*

Congratulations

You are now a *certified Sinclair BASIC Coder!*

Thank You for purchasing this book and taking the time to work through it. If you got through all the games you should be very familiar with BASIC by now, and able to write some programs of your own. Plan your games on paper first in rough form and then type in your code piece by piece.

I hope you had fun and learned a little along the way while you typed in some or all of these games. I hope you have enjoyed the experience and perhaps it has got your brain cells working on how to create super games of your own with Sinclair BASIC, or maybe you have been inspired to tackle other coding languages for your next project.

Don't forget to check out our Android games too, just search for Gazzapper Games on Playstore. Please leave a review for this book on store you purchased from.

You can follow us on www.Twitter.com/Gazzapper or visit our site and signup for updates
www.gazzapper.com

Thank you,
Gary Plowman

APPENDIX A - The character set

This is the complete Spectrum character set, with codes in decimal.

E.g. PRINT CHR$(38) will display the & character

Code	Character				
0	Not used	18	FLASH control	37	%
1	Not used	19	BRIGHT control	38	&
2	Not used	20	INVERSE control	39	,
3	Not used			40	(
4	Not used	21	OVER control	41	)
5	Not used	22	AT control	42	*
6	PRINT comma	23	TAB control	43	+
7	EDIT	24	Not used	44	,
8	←	25	Not used	45	-
9	→	26	Not used	46	.
10	↓	27	Not used	47	/
11	↑	28	Not used	48	0
12	DELETE	29	Not used	49	1
13	ENTER	30	Not used	50	2
14	number	31	Not used	51	3
15	not used	32	space	52	4
16	INK control	33	!	53	5
17	PAPER control	34	"	54	6
		35	#	55	7
		36	$		

56	8	79	O	102	F		
57	9	80	P	103	g		
58	:	81	Q	104	h		
59	;	82	R	105	i		
60	<	83	S	106	j		
61	=	84	T	107	k		
62	>	85	U	108	l		
63	?	86	V	109	m		
64	@	87	W	110	n		
65	A	88	X	111	o		
66	B	89	Y	112	p		
67	C	90	Z	113	q		
68	D	91	[	114	r		
69	E	92	/	115	s		
70	F	93	]	116	t		
71	G	94	^	117	u		
72	H	95	_	118	v		
73	I	96	£	119	w		
74	J	97	A	120	x		
75	K	98	B	121	y		
76	L	99	C	122	z		
77	M	100	D	123	{		
78	N	101	E	124				

125	}		147	(d)		170	SCREEN$	
126	~		148	(e)		171	ATTR	
127	©		149	(f)		172	AT	
128			150	(g)		173	TAB	
129	▪		151	(h)		174	VAL$	
130	▪		152	(i)		175	CODE	
131	▬		153	(j)		176	VAL	
132	▪		154	(k)		177	LEN	
133	▮		155	(l)		178	SIN	
134	▪▪		156	(m)		179	COS	
135	◤		157	(n)		180	TAN	
136	▪		158	(o)		181	ASN	
137	▪		159	(p)		182	ACS	
138	▮		160	(q)		183	ATN	
139	▙		161	(r)		184	LN	
140	▬		162	(s)		185	EXP	
141	◢		163	(t)		186	INT	
142	◣		164	(u)		187	SOR	
143	■		165	RND		188	SGN	
144	(a)		166	INKEY$		189	ABS	
145	(b)		167	PI		190	PEEK	
146	(c)		168	FN		191	IN	
			169	POINT		192	USR	

193	STR$	216	CIRCLE	239	LOAD
194	CHR$	217	INK	240	LIST
195	NOT	218	PAPER	241	LET
196	BIN	219	FLASH	242	PAUSE
197	OR	220	BRIGHT	243	NEXT
198	AND	221	INVERSE	244	POKE
199	<=	222	OVER	245	PRINT
200	>=	223	OUT	246	PLOT
201	<>	224	LPRINT	247	RUN
202	LINE	225	LLIST	248	SAVE
203	THEN	226	STOP	249	RANDOMIZE
204	TO	227	READ	250	IF
205	STEP	228	DATA	251	CLS
206	DEF FN	229	RESTORE	252	DRAW
207	CAT	230	NEW	253	CLEAR
208	FORMAT	231	BORDER	254	RETURN
209	MOVE	232	CONTINUE	255	COPY
210	ERASE	233	DIM		
211	OPEN #	234	REM		
212	CLOSE #	235	FOR		
213	MERGE	236	GO TO		
214	VERIFY	237	GO SUB		
215	BEEP	238	INPUT		

ABOUT THE AUTHOR

Gary Plowman is a Game Developer, Designer and Internet Entrepreneur from Dublin, Ireland. Gary Plowman founded Gazzapper Games in 2014 and to date his games have had millions of downloads.

It is November 1983 and young Billy Twist and his friends are about to discover the exciting new world of microcomputers and retro video games.

Take a trip into the 80s world of micros, 80s pop culture, BMX bikes, and classic video games in a story for 8-bit micro fans and geeks.

Printed in the USA
CPSIA information can be obtained
at www.ICGtesting.com
LVHW072006080124
768359LV00008B/897

9 780993 474453